THE ABSOLUTE CLASSICS

THE FOCUSED LIFE

including

LOVE'S MIRACLES

E. C. W. BOULTON

ELIM COMMUNICATIONS
and
NEW DAWN BOOKS

© Elim Communications 1995

The Focused Life *first published in November 1932*
Love's Miracles *first published in November 1931*

Reset with corrections in one volume May 1995

Published in the United Kingdom by

ELIM COMMUNICATIONS
P.O. Box 38, Cheltenham, Gloucester, GL50 3HN

and

NEW DAWN BOOKS
10A Jamaica Street, Greenock, Renfrewshire PA15 1YB

ISBN 1-870944-19-4

Typeset in the United Kingdom by
Peoples Print & Design, Birkenhead (Tel. 0151 691 2134)

Printed and bound in the United Kingdom by
The Guernsey Press, Channel Islands

CONTENTS

PUBLISHERS' PREFACE BY DEREK J. GREEN
Editor of Direction Magazine

Knowledge and wisdom are never obsolete. All that we know today is based on yesterday's knowledge. Wise people learn from yesterday, live today and plan for tomorrow.

Although the computer age has transported us into amazing realms of efficiency, and the information highway is opening up remarkable resources of knowledge, the human heart still longs to explore the spiritual realms which are unattainable by modern technology.

There is much to be learned from spiritual giants of any age. The words of Jesus Christ, Peter, Paul and John are just as relevant today as they were in Bible times. Similarly, the writings of a bygone generation can be enlightening and enriching for us today. Calvin and Luther are frequently quoted, while the writings of Spurgeon and Martyn Lloyd Jones are still top sellers.

One of yesterday's writers who has never been republished is E.C.W. Boulton. He was one of the great leaders of the Pentecostal Movement at the beginning of this century. He was a much loved pastor, an eloquent preacher who could draw the crowds, an inspiring, prohetic teacher, and a prolific writer with nearly twenty books to his name. His books have been out of print for many decades and consequently many of today's generation may not know of him. However, those who have stumbled on an old copy have been greatly blessed. We have even heard of people photocopying chapters and passing them around as if they were gold dust.

For some time those involved in Elim Publishing had felt that it was time to make these works available in a modern format so that thousands of Christians could benefit from his unique ministry and insight. During our consideration approaches were made by New Dawn Books asking for permission to do the same thing. This was taken as confirmation that the work should be done, and a joint publication is the result.

We are proud to present these two books in one at a price cheap by comparison with their original published price. In our presentation we have been faithful to the original style, retaining the King James version of Scripture wherever it was used. A few minor changes have been made where words or concepts have changed with the passing of time.

This double value volume will certainly transport the modern pressurised believer into a spiritual realm hitherto unknown.

FOREWORD BY WYNNE LEWIS
General Superintendent of Elim Pentecostal Churches

E.C.W. Boulton was one of the outstanding leaders that gave strong support to the fledgling Elim Churches founded by George Jeffreys at the beginning of this century. Mr. Boulton was the principal of the Elim Bible College during my student days in 1950/51. He was one of the nicest people I ever had the privilege to meet. He always seemed to live in heaven, and yet his feet were firmly on the ground. His Christian ministry began in the Salvation Army; after his baptism in the Holy Spirit he threw in his lot with the Elim Pentecostal Church and, from the early twenties on, he was an integral part of this dynamic thrust of the Holy Spirit in Great Britain. He was a prolific writer of both books and articles and was a hymn writer of note. Some of the best hymns sung in pentecostal churches today were from his pen. Those who heard the flow of his prophetic ministry were blessed indeed. He made an outstanding contribution to the growth of the Elim Pentecostal Church in those halcyon days. As a Bible college principal the students found him to be a father, earning the affectionate title "Pa Boulton"; he was a man of integrity, and one to whom we could always go with our problems. His counsel was wise and helpful. He was a great listener and, even in the midst of an extremely busy schedule, he always made time to handle people's personal problems.

During his ministry he held most of the highest offices in the Movement: Field Superintendent, Editor of the Elim Evangel and Principal of the Bible College.

During his lifetime, his books were in great demand, offering considerable inspiration and encouragement to the thousands of young converts at that time.

We believe that this reprint will prove as popular nowadays as at the beginning.

FOREWORD BY HUGH BLACK
**Founder Minister of Struthers Memorial Group of Churches
and Executive Director of New Dawn Books**

It is with great pleasure that I write a brief foreword for this book. I write on my own behalf and on behalf of the Struthers Memorial Group of Churches amongst whom Mr Boulton's memory is dearly cherished.

Over fifty years ago I had the privilege of being in a service in which Mr Boulton ministered. Towards the close I gave an utterance in tongues which he interpreted. I have never forgotten the moment. It seemed that living fire came above my head. I have never experienced anything quite like this either before or since.

In those days I was very young in Pentecost and I had a second memorable experience associated with Mr Boulton. My family were deeply opposed to our view of the baptism in the Holy Spirit and a family conference had been arranged for debate and discussion. On the previous day I had an injury at work which affected my hip and I found it very difficult to concentrate and study for the following night. At the critical point I was reading *A Ministry of the Miraculous* by Mr Boulton and suddenly, like a bolt from the blue, the thought came: "God could heal you now." It was immediately done. I was amazed. I changed chairs with my wife again and again – from high to low – but the pain was gone. I really was healed.

Finally, I would like to mention that a number of Mr. Boulton's devotional books such as *The Focused Life* and *Love's Miracles* are greatly valued in our fellowship and for many years now I feel as though people have almost begged, borrowed or "stolen" to satisfy the demand. I trust that a modern generation will find his works as acceptable as mine did.

THE FOCUSED LIFE

Holy, happy separation!
They alone are truly blest
Who from all besides retiring,
And Himself alone desiring,
Find in "Jesus only" rest.

Unto Thee! beloved Master,
Nearer, nearer let us be:
Unto Thee in consecration,
Unto Thee in separation,
Ever, only, unto Thee!

PREFACE TO THE FIRST EDITION

WITH deep thankfulness to God for the blessing which has rested upon three little volumes of heart talks already published, we now send forth this fourth volume in the hope that it may also find its way into the hands of many more who crave closer union with their risen Lord.

The writer will be happy indeed should he succeed in these pages in drawing some disheartened, despairing soul into the place of deep rest and victory in God. These talks are but the heart-breathings of one who is himself a seeker after more of the inexhaustible fulness of wealth treasured up in Christ. "Deeper yet" must ever be the heart-cry of those who have caught a glimpse "within the veil" of His exceeding glory.

And so it is to those who hunger and thirst after the Great Satisfier Himself that these pages are addressed – to those who, whilst they know Him, yet yearn to know Him in ever deepening intimacy.

E.C.W.B.
September 1932

Taken up with Jesus, filled and satisfied,
Conscious of His presence round on every side;
Many throng about me, yet the hush within
Stills the voice of passion, stays the power of sin.

Taken up with Jesus! with Himself alone,
Undivided kingdom, undivided throne!
He Himself, none other, I alone with Him,
'Neath the Shekinah glory and the cherubim.

THE FOCUSED LIFE

Fix your attention on . . . Jesus. – Hebrews iii. 1 (A S. Way).

I heard Him call, Come, follow;
That was all.
The world grew dim:
My soul went after Him.
I rose and followed – that was all –
Who would not follow if they heard Him call.

THE searchlight of God's holiness was focused on the life of a profligate African youth. So great was the agony it caused that his whole soul was shaken with the violence of his inward conflict. He longed to break away from his life of evil habits and evil friends. He was sitting one day with his friends in silence. "When deep reflection had brought together and heaped all my misery in the sight of my heart, there arose a mighty storm of grief, bringing a mighty shower of tears." He had to leave his friend to weep alone. He threw himself under a fig tree, and cried in despair, "How long? how long? To-morrow, to-morrow? Why not now? Why is there not this hour an end to my uncleanness?" – "So I was speaking and weeping in the contrition of my heart, when lo! I heard from a neighbouring house a voice as of a child, chanting and oft repeating, 'Take up and read, take up and read.' Instantly my countenance altered. I began to think whether children were wont to sing in play such words as these. So checking my tears, I rose, taking it to be a command from God to open the Book, and read the first chapter I should find." He returned to his friend, picked up a volume of Paul's Epistles, and in silence read the first verse on which his eyes rested, "Not in rioting and drunkenness . . ." "No further could I read, nor needed I. Instantly, at the end of this sentence, by a serene light infused into my soul, all the darkness of doubt vanished away."

The Focused Life

Augustine's life became focused upon Christ, and the profligate African youth became the most illustrious saint of the Western Church. The light was painful, but it revealed the sin within. The Saviour spoke, and it was henceforth upon Him that his life had become truly focused. The Christ held his vision, and all other things faded into insignificance.

It was on the Damascus road that the blinding vision of the glorious Christ broke upon Paul. From that moment his life became focused to a new centre. From that point throughout the whole of his subsequent career his being knew no other captivation. It is very beautiful to trace years after how his vision became clearer and yet more clear as he approached the time when the "darkling veil" would be exchanged for the "face to face" revelation. Growth in holiness, and life coming more clearly into spiritual focus can be measured by the acuteness of the consciousness of sin. The more our eyes take in His holiness, the more our deep sinfulness comes to view. The apostle's experience provides a striking commentary upon this aspect of truth.

In the year 59, writing to the Corinthians, Paul calls himself "the least of the apostles." Five years later in the year 64, writing to the Ephesians, he calls himself "less than the least of all saints," and in the year 65, when just finishing his course and ready to enter his Master's joy, he writes to Timothy and calls himself "the chief of sinners."

It is most important for the child of God to apprehend at the onset of his Christian career that he has been chosen and called to be conformed to the image of Christ, that his redeemed body is intended to become the sphere of Divine manifestation – that therein may be displayed the manifold virtues and glories of the Lord Jesus. Surely the goal as well as the guerdon of Christian discipleship must always be likeness to Him. Says the inspired writer, "Glorify God in your body," and "That the life . . . of Jesus might be made manifest in our body." "*Fix your attention on . . . Jesus!*" This means that all of life will be glorified as we catch the vision of Him. Look until the image of the Master is stamped upon the soul – look until this becomes the habit of the heart – look until all other spells are broken – until the whole being acknowledged the lordship of Christ.

For only as thou gazest
Upon the matchless beauty of His face,
Canst thou become a living revelation
Of His great heart of love, His untold grace.

Dr A. B. Simpson tells how on one occasion his little child

came to him and said: "Papa, look at that golden sign across the street a good while; now look at that brick wall and tell me what you see." "Why," said the father, "I see the golden sign on the brick wall." And the child laughed merrily over it. Only a simple story, but it suggests a great spiritual principle. It is the love-glued eyes that behold the beautiful in everything, and in which the beautiful finds expression.

Let us observe that spiritual focus is vital to the development of Christian character. In the second Epistle to the Corinthians, the third chapter and the eighteenth verse, Paul furnishes us with a picture of a soul in perfect focus. "All of us, with unveiled faces, reflecting like bright mirrors, the glory of the Lord, are being transformed into the same likeness, from one degree of radiant holiness to another, even as derived from the Spirit of the Lord." This indicates unobscured vision – nothing between to impair the outlook or the uplook. Nothing to dim the resplendent glory of Him upon whom the gaze of the soul is fixed.

In photography focus is vital – without it material is wasted, labour is lost, and results are unsatisfactory. No matter how perfect the apparatus employed, how beautiful the scene in view, let the question of focus be ignored or overlooked, and failure, with its attendant disappointment, must invariably and inevitably follow. That beautiful, sharp, clear image is often obtained by ever such a slight adjustment of the camera.

How quickly the delineation of the Divine upon the sensitive film of the human life may be rendered indistinct by a false attitude of the heart. A murmuring spirit will spoil the reflection of the heavenly radiance; a criticising disposition will cast a cloud over the whole life, taking the sweetness from the testimony. It is only as the believer maintains that position of complete abandonment to every known command of God that the life will become and remain a correct expression of the Divine thought. We must not forget that there is creative power in the God-planned life – He gives to that life a measure of the power of reproduction.

Alas, how many Christian lives are obviously out of focus. Fogged by some secret reservation which challenges the sovereignty of Christ. Overcast by the influence of some unshattered idol which is slowly but surely stealing the heart's allegiance from Jesus. Darkened by some unsanctified pursuit which threatens to grieve the Holy Spirit. These are some of the causes of that dim and defective portrayal of Christ. What a great need there is to guard against all those things that would draw us from our position of union and identification with our great Centre and Head.

The Focused Life

My Master, lead me to Thy door;
Pierce this now willing ear once more:
Thy bonds are freedom; let me stay
With Thee, to toil, endure, obey.

We are told by the naturalist that on their native rocks and ledges Alpine flowers are specially rich and gorgeous. The deep blue of the gentians, as well as crimson, rich reds, purple, gold-yellow, and pure white are scattered in lavish profusion. Lowland flowers when transferred to Alpine gardens at six hundred feet become richer and deeper and more vivid in colour. The reverse is equally true, for these mountaineers are neither so gorgeous, nor so rich planted in the lowlands as on their native rocks and ledges; their colour fades, their glory is lost, is it not thus with the soul out of focus and fellowship with God? Human nature has lost. Its sweetness, its richness, and its radiance, because it has stepped out of union with God.

Let us notice further that true spiritual focus is vital to a successful service-life. John xv. 5 serves to reveal this. "He that abideth in Me, and I in him, the same bringeth forth much fruit." Here again we see that the quality of service is determined by the attitude of the servant to his Master. A law of relationship which governs the issues of service must be recognised and obeyed. Just as the fruit is produced and perfected by the cooperative action of the earth and the sun, so the life of the believer must be lived in utmost harmony with all those Divine forces which are responsible for its productiveness. Let any influence be introduced which sways the soul out of focus, and speedily fruitfulness is affected. The generative power is arrested - the life is removed from its true source and centre, and though its activities may be continued, and even increased, yet it is powerless to perform its appointed function in the purpose of God. It requires readjustment; it is out of sympathetic and vital relationship with that upon which it is entirely dependent. Again, on the other hand, if the Christian realises the importance of having his life regulated to the Divine requirements, and moreover, carefully respects those principles which govern relationship to God in service, then to what blessed results this may lead in ministry.

We have but to listen to the testimony of one or two of God's servants whose service has been so signally blessed, to realise that the vital experience that has made them so fruitful was when their lives were brought into focus with Jesus Christ as their one objective.

A. B. Simpson tells how he learnt the secret of a focused life. Many and long and bitter were his struggles to hold fast his healing, to cling to his sanctification, to grip his faith. In spite of all his efforts, perhaps because of them, he seemed to lose everything, till in despair he felt he had no faith at all. How tenderly God spoke to him then, "Never mind, my child. You have nothing; but I am Perfect Power, I am Perfect Love, I am Faith, I am your Life, I am the preparation for the Blessing, and then I am the Blessing too. I am all within, and all without, and all for ever."

In those beautiful lines which A. B. Simpson penned we see how completely the centre of his life's focus was changed:

> *Once it was the blessing,*
> *Now it is the Lord;*
> *Once it was the feeling,*
> *Now it is His Word;*
>
> *Once His gifts I wanted,*
> *Now the Giver own;*
> *Once I sought for healing,*
> *Now Himself alone.*

Another man whose work for the Lord has been richly blessed tells a similar story of how his spiritual life was brought to a crisis. Dr. Trumbull, the well-known American writer, had been championing the very cause of the highest possible conception of Christ by conducting in the columns of the *Sunday School Times* a symposium on the deity of Christ, in which the leading Bible scholars of the world were testifying. In spite of all his efforts, his struggles and his profession, his spiritual life was a failure; there was no fruit, no victory over besetting sins, and he felt he did not know the Jesus Christ of whom he wrote. In his little book, *The Life that Wins*, he tells the story of the great change. At the Edinburgh World Missionary Conference he went to hear an address on "The Resources of the Christian Life." He went eagerly expecting to be told a series of definite things to do to strengthen the Christian life. The first words showed him his mistake and made his heart leap with a new joy. "The resources of the Christian life, my friends, are just . . . Jesus Christ." On his knees Dr. Trumbull fought it out till he could truly say, "To me to live is Christ." He says, "God, in His long suffering patience, forgiveness, and love, gave me . . . a new Christ, wholly new in the conception and consciousness of Christ that now became mine." His life now being focused became fruitful.

To get out of harmony with the will of God means a loss of spiritual proportion and perspective. How many there are, even within the ranks of the redeemed, who place the trivial in the foreground of their outlook upon life. They emphasise the secondary and overlook the primary. They are concerned with the label which the goods bear rather than the goods themselves. They will go to any amount of trouble to make the external orthodox, and pay but scant attention to the weightier matters relating to the right adjustment of the life's true centre. They will insist upon devoting themselves most assiduously to the circumference of things. To them the visible is the vital. And so often times the highest and the best is missed. Blessed indeed are those souls who possess this spiritual sense which enables them to choose the choicest and hold fast to the utmost. Unless we are endued with this spiritual perception, we shall often find ourselves deceived in our estimate of men and things. To those Christ-focused souls comes the keen-sightedness which permits them to detect the real gold beneath the rough exterior – to their trained ear the false ring of the coin is at once apparent – no glittering trappings can hide the nakedness and hollowness of that which is not Divine in its character.

Furthermore we see that true spiritual focus is indispensable to a powerful prayer life. "If ye abide in Me, and My words abide in you, ye shall ask what ye will, and it shall be done." Freedom in prayer characterises the focused soul; God can entrust it with powers and privileges which will not be misused or abused. The human will becomes so completely dominated and driven by Divine love, that there is no fear of false petition. "What ye will," is always in perfect accord with the will of God; the prayer power of the focused life is spent in bringing to pass the plan of God; the soul is so thoroughly adjusted that the necessity for restriction in the prayer sphere is removed and the utmost liberty is allowed. As S. D. Gordon so beautifully expresses it, "When God can reach in His hand and do as He likes with us, we can reach out our hands and do as we like with – God!" It appears on the surface to be a tremendous thing to say, but the more carefully it is examined, the clearer becomes the conviction that it is exactly the line upon which God works.

The life becomes so attuned to its environment in God that even the breath of desire is dynamic with creative energy – the thought-life is so dominated by the Holy Spirit that it functions freely in harmony with the Divine will. Aspirations become Christ-captivated.

We remember reading of a certain medieval believer whose reputation for saintliness was so great that numbers flocked to her, seeking her prayers on their behalf. She listened to their requests, but quickly forgot all about them – so occupied was she in the contemplation of her Lord. Great was her astonishment, therefore, when day after day people came to thank her for the benefits and blessings received through the medium of her prayers, But as she considered this unusual thing, she suddenly saw its significance. She had been in such close union with the Source of help and healing – that without conscious effort, from her love-charged life, had overflowed the benediction and balm so much needed by those eager seekers.

We too may live in such intimate and uninterrupted union with our great living Head that from our redeemed lives may flow, spontaneous and free,

A stream of tenderness and grace –
Loving, because God loved, eternally.

He is altogether lovely, better is His love than wine;
Tender, infinitely human, Jesus gloriously Divine!
And the world cries shame upon Him,
But from Christ I shall not part –
His in life and death, for ever,
And His home is in my heart.

HIS LOVELINESS

His speech is the very perfection of sweetness! And Himself the concentration of loveliness. – Song of Solomon v. 16 (Spurrell).

> *Led captive by His sweetness,*
> *And dowered with His bliss,*
> *For ever He is ours,*
> *For ever we are His.*

WHAT a priceless privilege is thine, O child of God! With anointed vision to behold Him in whom all the Divine fulness resides and is revealed! He whose glory exceeds that of the noonday sun, and in whom all the Divine attributes find their fullest expression! Drawn by His hand into the "inner court" of intimate communion, there to listen to "the thrilling music of His voice," and have "His fragrance poured upon thee."

It is not difficult to distinguish those who have lingered long in the Divine presence – a few moments in their company is sufficient to reveal the fact that they "have been alone with Jesus." There is a glory which cannot be veiled – a sweetness and gentleness which cannot be concealed – a fragrance which pervades and permeates the whole life, giving to it an almost irresistible power of attraction. Thus beholding Him, life becomes –

> *An endless heaven of love,*
> *A rapture, and a glory, and a calm;*
> *. . . An everlasting Psalm.*

We recently read the following account of an interesting event connected with Scottish history. It was in 1745 that Charles Stuart landed in Scotland, and the chieftains commenced to rally to his standard. It is related of Lochiel that he had no faith in the enterprise, and that he informed his brother that he would go and expostulate with the prince. His brother's advice was: "Go not near the prince, for so fascinating is the power of his person, that he will toss your mind like a feather in the wind, and you will be unable to do what you wish." Lochiel, however, would not be dissuaded. He went and saw the prince, who listened patiently to his remonstrances and then replied: "My father hath often told me how that Lochiel in the days gone by hath done brave deeds for his king, and tomorrow the standard will be raised, and you will go to your home, and at your fireside will learn the fortunes or fate of your prince." Then the chieftain, deeply moved, answered, "The standard will be raised and I will be there, and every man of my clan will pour out to the last drop his blood for the prince." Even so would those who have named the Name of Christ and who have come under His wondrous fascination, give themselves "to the last drop of blood" for the cause of their King.

Dear child of God, are you by nature hard and unyielding, and is there in your disposition that which repels? Betake yourself to the chamber of prayer and meditation, and tarry there until He speaks somewhat of His loveliness into your poor, cold, barren nature. Here in this place of revelation you shall exchange the spirit of heaviness for the garment of praise, and you shall come forth with "songs and everlasting joy upon your head." Take your difficulties, your burdens, your sorrows, those things which make your soul to smart, take them to Him; look upon His radiant beauty, and you shall find deliverance from your ills and woes.

Do you realise a resistance to the operation of the Holy Spirit, which threatens to thwart His plan for your life? A shrinking fear which prevents you from launching forth upon the promises and trusting yourself wholly to Jesus? Tarry awhile in His holy presence, and you shall discover that perfect love casts out all fear, and into your life there shall come a wonderful and blessed freedom, which will enable you to do the will of God with delight. In this place of "perfect good" you shall acquire –

> *The broken will,*
> *Which, leaning on Omnipotence,*
> *Is more than conqueror still.*

Here you shall find your tongue loosened in praise and prayer, and forth from your enraptured being shall issue a ceaseless stream of adoration both deep and strong.

O soul beset by fierce temptation, get you up to the mountain of vision, and there alone with God you shall learn the way to victory! Contemplate His strength until courage and confidence flow into your timid, faltering heart! Gaze upon His spotless purity until your iniquity is purged and your dross consumed, so that nothing but pure gold remains! Look upon Him until out of your nothingness shall emerge His own wonderful undertaking for you. Look away from what you are and what you have, and learn that your sufficiency is of God.

> *Look full in His wonderful face,*
> *And the things of earth will grow strangely dim*
> *In the light of His glory and grace.*

Is your heart still cold and sluggish, unresponsive and unmoved? It needs the Master's touch. "Gainsborough, the artist, a master in his own sphere, was for ever yearning to be a musician, and in turn bought quite a variety of musical instruments, and attempted to play them with but moderate success. Hearing the master Giardini at Bath play the violin and produce some ravishing music, Gainsborough was thrown into such transports of admiration and envy that he was frantic until he had bought Giardini's instrument. Great was his surprise and chagrin, however, when he found that the musical charm remained with the Italian, and the instrument itself was nothing – the kind of player was everything. It is the touch of the master which makes the instrument speak with such heart-thrilling powers." Come into His banqueting chamber and feast upon His loveliness, and soon you will find your heart aglow with holy purpose and passion, and within you will be kindled the flame of an unquenchable love, and from the place of vision you shall go forth to the field of service, carrying with you somewhat of the glory of that inner sanctuary. You shall realise that you are in partnership with the eternal God – that you are yoked to Him by unbreakable love-bonds. See to it that you do not miss the mark for the prize of your high calling in Christ! Yield to all His inner working until "thy poor life be all Divine."

> *Communicate Thy sweetness*
> *Lord of love –*
> *Turn life's water into wine*
> *From above.*

Perhaps your life has many a twisted thread; like some tangled skein it lies a hopeless complication. Do not in your anxiety make matters worse – let the skilful hand of the Master Weaver unravel the tangled threads – out of the baffling confusion He will bring forth a

21

rich design, something beyond your utmost expectations. Go to the sanctuary, and as your soul gets into contact and correspondence with God, you shall understand – the mystery will be revealed in the light of His unsullied loveliness. As you gaze upon His incomparable beauty you will exclaim –

> *Work on then, Lord, till on my soul*
> *Eternal light shall break,*
> *And in Thy likeness perfected*
> *I satisfied shall wake.*

Perhaps nowhere can the soul command a clearer or truer vision of the love and loveliness of Jesus than that which breaks forth in dazzling splendour from the Cross. There in those magnificent moments – so pregnant with soul agony – shone the glory of the Christ; through His humiliating suffering, in blood-red radiance, beamed the inexpressible sweetness of Divine grace and love. If Galilee and Gennesaret reveal the wondrous beauty of Jesus; if there amid the dark shades of earth's dusty highway we can discover somewhat of His glory, then surely His ineffable and incomparable loveliness finds its fullest expression on Calvary's tragic yet sublime height.

Here it was that His love seemed to burst through like a mighty river, bearing away on its bosom all the accumulated sin of a rebel world; it was as though the very sluice gates of love had been lifted to let through the redemptive energy of God.

It is the Spirit-spoken vision and call of the Cross that lays the guilt-stricken soul at the Redeemer's feet in love's glorious bondage, never to go out free again; for ever the love-slave of Him who gave Himself utterly and to the uttermost. Before such beauty the soul sinks in eternal surrender, asking no greater bliss than to follow whithersoever He leads.

O Lover of my soul, possess and fill the earthen mould with the Treasure Divine! Take this poor vase of clay and make it the receptacle of Thine unsearchable riches! Lead Thou me into the sweet mysteries of Love's power! Show me the secrets of the inner chamber where Love unveils and unburdens itself! Let me be the partner of Thy kingdom!

O Dawn most fair! O Day most bright!
Across the eastern sky
The Advent glory soon shall break –
Redemption draweth nigh.

It may be sooner than we think
Shall end the long delay!
It may be that the Bridegroom-King
E'en now is on His way!

FACE TO FACE

So now we see darkly, by a mirror, but then face to face.
I Cor. xiii. 12 (Conybeare and Howson).

Jesus, these eyes have never seen
That radiant form of Thine;
The veil of sense hangs dark between
Thy blessed face and mine.

WHAT a magnificent note of assurance this passage possesses. It is one of those full-chorded harmonies of inspiration that rouse the soul to inexpressible raptures. It indicates the writer to be a man of unclouded faith.

What sweet sequence these words contain – " Now . . . then!" Today the vision partial and preliminary; tomorrow perfect and permanent. Yet today's vision is blessedly progressive, growing fuller and clearer as our spiritual capacity is enlarged. Moreover today's vision is preparatory to the wider unveiling of tomorrow. The glory of the future would prove too great for the present – we could not bear it now. The darkened glass is necessary to our present state; without it we could have no vision of His glory. And so actually it is to us the friendly medium of revelation.

"But then face to face!" It is the prospect of the beloved who looks onward to the hour of consummated hope and love. It is the contemplation of one in whose breast burns the confidence of reunion – whose pulse beats high with the thought of meeting her beloved. Standing on the mountain's brow and gazing with love-quickened vision across the "little while" between, she catches sight of the rosy-tinted dawn – to her faith-illumined heart the heavens are pregnant with promise. She descries on the distant horizon a glory that to other eyes is hidden; it is the coming of the Bridegroom – coming for His purchased possession, His peculiar treasure. Over the storm-swept

25

cloudland of earth, her vision soars to the far-off glory-lit summit of Olivet.

So much in life has been mantled in mystery. The human has tried in vain to peer into the "why and wherefore" of a thousand baffling and bewildering experiences. We have sought the unsealing of the secret things; we have coveted the interpretation of the unfathomable; in our eager quest we have cried, "Lord, lift the veil, break down the unseen barriers; admit us to the impenetrable; let us span the separating sea of sense, and learn the mysteries of existence." Why have we been called to drink of Marah's bitter waters? Why have we been allowed to tread the burning desert sands, and climb Golgotha's painful steep? Why have we been disciplined in the school of suffering? We have cried within ourselves, "My way is hidden from the Lord, and my judgment is passed over from my God."

Be patient, O my soul, when thou seest Him face to face, the inexplicable in life shall then find a full and satisfactory explanation. Then the veil of mystery shall be for ever pierced. With the friendly dawn of eternity shall come the unravelling of the midnight's mystery. Be of good comfort, one of these days thy journey shall end; thou shalt compass the last mile and climb the final summit, and upon thy longing eyes shall break the face-to-face vision of thy Lord.

"Then face to face." Perhaps this supplies the greatest incentive to dare and do for God. This kindling vision awakes within us a new and stronger impulse to holiness – it beckons us on to the unrealised and unpossessed – it invites us to compass the utmost. It may not be ours to live brilliantly, but with such a stimulus we may live bravely and boldly, even in the face of the fiercest winds that blow across the pathway of the Christian pilgrim. We may hold our heads high with holy pride, as we anticipate that advent hope. Life will be invested with a new nobility – a fresh fervour – a deeper devotion, when we contemplate that veil-less meeting with our risen Lord.

> *We wait and watch and wrestle –*
> *The way too dark to trace:*
> *But all will turn to glory when*
> *We see Thy face.*

"Then face to face." It is the goal at the end of the race – the garland of victory at the close of the conflict – the prize for patient perseverance - the all-satisfying recognition for a life of diligent discipleship.

This then was the hope that animated the heart of that early

Church. She had ceased to look for an earthly paradise – her anchorage was no longer in the temporal. Her vision – trained by the Divine Spirit – was outward and upward. Worldliness had loosed its hold of her life – her affections were centred upon things above. She marched to an Advent air – moved amid an Advent atmosphere – was permeated and possessed by the Advent spirit.

Alas, is not this all too often the lost chord in the music of the modern evangel? There is no radiant expectancy – no joyous anticipation – no buoyant belief – all the creation of this Gospel of the returning Christ.

> *Hasten, Lord, Thy coming,*
> *Quicken now my pace;*
> *Soon shall come the time when*
> *I shall see Thy face.*

"Face to face." This most surely implies recognition. I shall know Him in that day. He will be distinguishable from all others, though they be ten thousand times ten thousand in number. My clarified vision will pick out the One who ransomed me at the cost of His own wonderful life. No other being can ever displace Him in that hour in the eyes of those who are privileged to behold His glory. And then too I shall be like Him – this body of my humiliation shall be fashioned like unto the body of His glory. As we have borne the image of the earthy, so shall we also bear the image of the heavenly. What a blessed destiny for the believer in Christ. The corruptible changed for the incorruptible. The shadows of eventide turned into the full blaze of eternal noontide. Our mantle of mortality discarded for the vesture of immortality. Our *"light affliction"* replaced by the *"eternal weight of glory."*

For ever clothed in the beauty of His holiness – visibly and consciously robed in His radiant righteousness.

O Thou Divine Lover of my soul, let this vision of Thy coming eclipse all earth-centred dreams! Let it master me in the morning of life, nourish me in life's noontide, and should the evening shadows gather about me, then let its glory still envelop me. Let it be the wordless song of my soul in life's deep and eloquent silences, when the hush of a great awe possesses my spirit, as I meditate upon that tearless morn. Make all nature vibrant with the rich harmony of Thine appearing. Command the winds that they whisper the message of Thine epiphany. Speak unto the trees of the field that they proclaim Thy nearness. Let the waves of the sea announce Thy advent, and every hill and dale re-echo with the glad refrain, "Behold, the Bridegroom cometh!"

Blessed Spirit, Thou who gavest birth to this heart-enthralling hope, kindle afresh each day its flame upon the altar of my heart. Let it glow with inextinguishable and undiminishing glory within the temple of my being. Make me to rise each morning with the advent music ringing within the sanctuary of my soul. Cause mine eyes to catch the streaks of light upon the distant horizon, blessed tokens of Thine appearing – heralds and harbingers of that morn without clouds. Make all my little world brimful of the golden beauty of Thy coming – let me live on the tip-toe of expectation, so that when Thou dost cleave the clouds I may rise to join Thee in the radiant air.

Then shall the desert blossom as the rose, and become as the garden of the Lord – in the wildrness shall refreshing streams rise, and even the waste and barren places shall develop into fruitfulness. All life shall be purged and purified by this hope enthroned within. Even the commonplace shall be possessed of a new loveliness, and life's lowliest vales shall be luminous with the wonder of this living hope. When mine eyes see all things in the light of this expectation, then shall I give to them a wise and true interpretation; I shall read aright the meaning of the manifold mysteries which clamour for explanation; in the language of current events I shall discover the fulfilment of prophetic vision; upon the scroll of time I shall see written the things which announce Thine appearing.

In the advent light, O Saviour,
I am living day by day:
Waiting, working, watching ever,
Knowing Thou art on Thy way.

See the advent glory breaking!
Faith will soon be lost in sight:
"Face to face" I shall behold Him –
Bathed in His eternal light!

Go! Wait before Him where His voice may reach thee,
Wait where His touch may thrill thee through and through —
Until His glorious face shall shine upon thee,
With grace and love undreamed of hitherto.
The lingering light of God's own gracious presence;
His voice, His touch, still giving strength to thee.

THE TOUCH DIVINE

And Jesus came and touched them. – Matt. xvii. 7.

> *In the still air the music lies unheard,*
> *In the rough marble beauty hides unseen,*
> *To make the music and the beauty*
> *Needs a master's touch, the sculptor's chisel keen.*
> *Great Master, touch us with Thy skilled hand,*
> *Let not the music that is in us die,*
> *Great Sculptor, hew and polish us,*
> *Nor let, hidden and lost, Thy form within us die.*

ONLY a touch! And yet what a wealth of meaning may be conveyed in this way. In most lives there are those rare occasions when a single touch is more eloquent than words. Times when the language of the lips is exhausted, and the finest feelings of the heart flow through the channel of direct personal contact. Have we not, when passing through the bitterness of some sudden and staggering bereavement, when the heart has been numbed with grief, felt the value of a tender touch? It was only the mute pressure of a loving hand, 'tis true, but how much it meant to us in that dark hour of loss, when our soul was curtailed in night. Perchance it told us of another who came alongside to be the partner of our pain. Perhaps 'twas but a touch of a falling tear of one who was weeping with us, but it brought sweet comfort to our aching heart. "They say that if a piano is struck in a room where another one stands unopened and untouched, who lays his ear to that will hear a string within, as if touched by the hand of some shadowy spirit, sound the same note. But more strange, how the strings of one heart vibrate with those of another; how woe awakens woe; how grief infects with sadness; how sympathy may be so delicate and acute as to become a pain." If this applies to human friendships, how much more is the union of the soul with Him whose love is so exquisite and eternal. Yes, it is in the night of adversity that the touch of Jesus is most real and precious.

There is grace and power for the trying hour
By the touch of the hand Divine.

"He touched her . . . and she arose." Has not the quickening touch of Jesus thus come to us when down in some deep slough of despond or away under some juniper tree of unbelief, lifting us into the gladdening sunshine of eternal hope? That touch has caused fresh fountains of praise to rise within the soul, giving strength for new endurance and endeavour, and awakening new spiritual aspirations and ambitions. Who can tell the transport of those transforming touches upon the inner life? Moments when "deep calleth unto deep," and the sweet incense of His presence fills the sanctuary of the soul. That touch unseals the alabaster box of our heart's love till it pours itself out for others who dwell amidst earth's shadows and sorrows. Only a touch. Yes, but what a difference it may make in a human life. See yonder opal as it lies among other precious stones, how dull and lustreless it appears. But take it in your hand for a moment, and observe the change produced. Now it gleams and flashes with all the glories of the rainbow. Ah, it was the warm touch of a human hand which brought forth the latent loveliness. Is this not exactly what takes place in our lives when touched by Jesus? That mystic touch sets the joy-chords vibrating once more. At that wonderful touch there breaks forth in our lives a flame of fervent love which makes them glow with a new spiritual splendour, and invests them with the glory of a new creation. And then to think of the infinite tenderness of that touch Divine. Gentleness ever characterised the ministry of Christ – He lays His hand upon life's deepest wounds and they are healed. Dr. Jowett says, "Real gentleness is not weakened strength; it is strength disciplined, purified, refined. Gentleness is matured strength." What might and tenderness are blended in the touch of the nail-pierced Hands.

The living touch of the living Christ
Always new life bestows.

"Let loose the angel," said Michael Angelo as he looked at a great block of marble. Taking the sculptor's chisel and hammer he cut away great flakes, and laboured until one of his glorious statues was to be seen. "It is only the eye of the sculptor that can see beforehand the finished statue in the rough marble block; but he does see it, and all the strokes of his tool are meant to bring out to the eyes of others what is already clear to his own. Blessed blows that fall upon us at times from the hand of the great Sculptor – all with a view to the perfecting of His own wondrous image in us. Touches that leave us purer and nobler and more like the Lord.

Only a touch. Yes, but is this not expressive of tender *intimacy*? All the old "middle walls of partition" are gone – no longer any strangeness exists 'twixt my Lord and me. That precious freedom, which is the fragrant fruit of friendship, now characterises our communion. No need of words now, a touch is sufficient to disclose the hidden meaning of the heart – that gentle, almost imperceptible, spiritual pressure tells in unspoken yet unmistakable terms the secret of His incomparable love, causing our love to flow back to Him in richer, fuller, purer intensity.

> *My faith looks up to claim that touch Divine*
> *Which robs me of this fatal strength of mine,*
> *And leaves me trusting wholly, Lord, on Thine.*

Again the touch of the Master denotes *proximity*. It is the inaudible yet wondrously intelligible assurance, "Lo, I am with you," which restores our exhausted energies and renews life's lost harmonies. It reminds us that He walks with us "along life's rugged road," the changeless Companion of all its vicissitudes – our Emmanuel. When swept by some swift tornado of temptation, that touch tells me that God is "at hand" in His unsleeping love to minister to my needs; He is there to still my heart's alarms and turn my travail to triumph.

> *Thy need His touch can meet, –*
> *The touch of the living, loving Christ –*
> *Go, seek it at His feet.*

"He touched her . . . and the fever left her." So many Christian lives are full of fever of various kinds. Think of the fever of fear, how impotent it renders the believer who comes under its enervating influence. Ah, 'tis the Jesus touch that can extract that harmful feverishness which so mars the life and testimony of the child of God; just a touch from Him who calmed the boisterous billows will bring the soul into the haven of unutterable gladness and undisturbed repose. Turn to Him, dear distressed and distraught soul, and let thy weary head pillow itself upon the bosom of His boundless love; thus thou shalt realise and respond to the thrill of the Divine touch which shall adjust thy life to His perfect and wonderful will.

That touch may come to you in the shape of test. "We understand that there are two methods of testing metals. One is known as the 'impact' test in which fracture of the testpiece is effected by a single blow; the other is the 'fatigue' test, in some forms of which millions of repetitions of comparatively small stresses are required. We believe that the latter method is considered the most searching and severe."

Who can estimate the tremendous dynamic of the Divine touch? Life becomes infused with a new enthusiasm which dominates and directs all the activities of the soul, endowing it with an unconquerable courage and grace that carry it out into the "vast and shoreless deep" of a life completely swallowed up in God. Let Him touch thy lips, and thou shalt speak and sing with the authority which that touch alone can give. Let Him but touch thy ears, and they shall be attuned to catch the slightest whisper of His will. Let thine eyes receive the Jesus touch, and thou shalt behold wondrous things in His Word; the mysteries of God shall unfold themselves to thy clarified vision. Thus touched by the hand of the Lord –

More than conqueror in the strength Divine,
Into thee God's radiance now can shine.

Utterly abandoned to the Holy Ghost!
Seeking all His fulness at whatever cost;
Cutting all the shorelines, launching in the deep
Of His mighty power – strong to save and keep.

Utterly abandoned to the Holy Ghost!
Oh! the sinking, sinking, until self is lost!
Until the emptied vessel lies broken at His feet;
Waiting till His filling shall make the work complete.

GOD'S TENDER CARE

As an eagle stirs its nestlings, fluttering over its brood . . .
so the Eternal alone was their leader.
Deut. xxxii. 11, 12 (Moffatt).

Underneath us, oh how easy,
We have not to mount on high,
But to sink into His fulness,
And in trustful weakness lie.
And we find our humbling failures
Save us from the strength that harms;
We may fail, but underneath us,
Are the everlasting Arms.

WE have read the description of the eagle feeding its young, and how the mother bird teaches her eaglet to fly. A rocky ledge on the sheer face of the cliff or precipice, a nest of twigs lined with soft wool from the sheep, is the home of the king of birds. The little ones are loth to leave their place of safety and launch out upon the air into the depths beneath. Entreaties are of no avail, and even tempting food held before the hungry little one fails to lure it from its safe home. The mother bird, when she finds every other device has failed, determines on more desperate methods. Dropping from above him with one mighty swoop she sweeps nest and eaglet off the rocky ledge out into the dizzy depths. The little one flaps wildly for dear life, sometimes the effort to fly grows more and more wild till he loses his balance and falls headlong into the depths beneath. Not for one moment has the mother left him – on tireless wing she hovers around him, and now she swoops beneath him, and the little one falls on to her strong back, rights himself, and when she drops from under him again, is able to fly to the treetops below where the proud mother feeds her tired but triumphant offspring.

In Israel of old we see God's eaglet. "As an eagle!" It is a simple and beautiful simile. The eagle's eyrie is in a dangerous spot on the face of some precipice. The nestling place which God chose for the rearing of his chosen people Israel was as unexpected as it was dangerous, among a people who would naturally be expected to be their enemies. But though the nest was of thorns, Jehovah lined it soft and warm for His brood; Egypt became the home of the Israelites in a most dramatic manner. The story of Joseph shows us the great Disposer of circumstances weaving His plans to attain this particular purpose, and is a masterpiece of strategy beyond man's imagination. The nest was lined, Israel was given the best of the land of Egypt, and throve and multiplied, till the time came when Jehovah knew it was the moment for His eaglet to fly.

"As an eagle stirreth up her nest!" As long as the nest is so comfortable the little bird will not learn to fly. The comforts that were so good for its childhood are not suitable for strong growth. It always goes against the grain when babes, natural or racial or spiritual, have to learn the uncomfortable lesson that the time has come for them to launch out and learn to use their pinions. "A king arose who knew not Joseph," and here begins another series of events of an opposite kind which the great Disposer arranges to bring His people out of Egypt. The great persecution of the Israelites by the Egyptians, which aimed at checking their growth in numbers, only seemed to have the effect of making them more fertile. Slavery must have developed in them a capacity for hard work and strong endurance that stood them in good stead in their wilderness journey. Moses, by his action, removes the last of any soft lining to their nest that might have remained, and when the promise of the land to be their very own and the accompanying entreaties have failed, the nest is stirred till the thorns make it an impossible abode. The plagues of Egypt ended with that last and terrible death of the firstborn. The Egyptians, desperate in their loss, turn round and almost force their slaves out of their land. The Passover night and the exodus from Egypt are a stepping out in faith of God's chosen people, resting on His pledge of the promised land. God's eaglet is afloat on the air!

The heavenlies are the true element of the spiritually-minded believer. "In heavenly places in Christ Jesus." "Our conversation is in heaven." To soar is our birthright. "They shall mount up with wings as eagles." Truly to claim our heritage in the heavenlies, however, is no mean achievement. God would fain teach His children how to dwell in the upper heights of fellowship with Him. To enjoy this wing life we must rely no longer on our rocky ledge – we must learn to launch out into the infinite and the invisible.

God's Tender Care

Launch out on the Divine,
Draw from His love-filled store.
Trust Him with everything;
Begin to-day,
And find the joy that comes
When Jesus has His way.

What an uncomfortable feeling it is! Our home no longer a refuge; everything seems to have been spoilt; thorny circumstances arise that penetrate an all sides, till we are so uncomfortable we would gladly get out, but fear of the future makes us cling with all our might to the old. The place which we once felt to be so vital to our well-being we will at last gladly exchange for the place of His choice. Then there comes over us a kind of premonition that God is calling us. We commence to see and feel quite clearly what it all means, but the fear of the depths is upon us. Then comes an awful upheaval and in some crisis or climax we are launched out into the abyss. Full surrender, utter abandonment, whatever we may call it, is a desperate step, taken often in fear and trembling. There is a violent effort to right oneself, and a headlong fall follows, but it is a fall that flings us upon God the Father in a new and deeper sense than ever before. We discover that underneath us and around us are the omnipotent Arms of Jehovah.

It is a most extraordinary fact that man will not learn to trust till he has exhausted all his own powers, and is brought to a place of desperate extremity. Again and again we have to learn the same lesson. When we have finished, God then steps in. We do not find out that underneath are the everlasting Arms till we fall into them. Exhausted with our desperate efforts at self-preservation, at last we sink down into what seems infinite space, but what actually proves to be the bosom of Eternal Love. God will wait until utter exhaustion throws us back upon the Inexhaustible and Eternal. He has determined that we should live together with Him the life of resurrection in the heavenlies. He has planned for us the life of the wing. It is impossible to reproduce in our own minds what a tremendous launching out in faith Hudson Taylor made when he started for China. It was the same when George Muller commenced his orphanage work. We are told that P. P. Bliss, the hymn writer, had been pressed by Moody to give up his life entirely to evangelistic work, but he hesitated. He decided he would have a trial mission to see how he got on. The first meeting was not encouraging. On the occasion of the second meeting it rained hard, and yet the numbers were doubled. A consciousness of responsibility came over the workers. Bliss made the full surrender plunge and yielded his musical ambitions, his writing of secular music, everything; and himself to God to be used in His service. That night they had a wonderful meeting; revival broke out, and Bliss himself became a veritable fountain of Gospel music.

Christmas Evans riding in the country felt the need of that plunge into full surrender's tide, and tethered his horse, while he walked up and down struggling with the coldness of his own heart. He made the leap, and next day a revival started that spread all over Wales.

Mrs. Booth-Clibborn knew what it meant that clay when she stood before her Brussels audience, clad in sackcloth, mourning for the sins of the people. They listened to her then as they would not to any other preacher of the Gospel. She had taken a leap in the dark that cost her intense agony. But she had learnt to throw herself utterly and irrevocably upon God, and she reaped a rich reward.

And so it is that we must learn to launch out upon the shoreless, boundless ocean of God's faithfulness and fulness. Whilst we cling to the visible we shall never know the deep full joy of the invisible and eternal – we shall never realise the peace and rest that possesses the being of those who feel beneath them God's almightiness, if we persist in holding to the temporal, and what appears to be the tangible.

Is it not worth while if in being brought to realise our natural bankruptcy, we discover the unfathomed and unfailing resources of the Eternal One? God is thus pushing us out into a new life of infinite possibility.

I grasp Thy strength, make it my own,
My heart with peace is blessed.
I lose my hold, and then comes down
Darkness and cold unrest.

Let me no more my comfort draw
From my frail hold of Thee;
In this alone rejoice with awe –
Thy mighty grasp of me.

He knoweth how to keep in perfect peace
The soul in which His reign doth never cease.
"No longer I, but Christ" — I may not choose,
But follow each command, nor e'er refuse
A call to service, whatsoe'er it be,
For Jesus calls — it is enough for me.
Oh, life of sweetest liberty so blest;
I yield Him all, and He does all the rest.

WILLING THRALLS

But now . . . you have become thralls to God.
Romans vi. 22 (A. S. Way).

PETER tells us in his second epistle that "a man is the slave of any one by whom he has been worsted in fight." Many of us – like Saul of Tarsus – fought against Christ in the old days; we struggled for supremacy, seeking to establish the sovereignty of self. But at last we found our resistance broken down – stronghold after stronghold fell before the omnipotent love of God, until eventually the central citadel of our being capitulated to Christ; we surrendered to Him the keys of the kingdom of life, and tendered Him the sword of rebellion. We discovered that Divine love is the mightiest dynamic in the world.

And so we have become "thralls to God" by reason and right of conquest. We are no longer our own; the ownership of life has been transferred to another; we are now vassals of a more glorious Master; bondslaves of a more worthy monarch.

And as we have borne the marks of our former suzerain, self and sin, so now we carry the insignia of a new service; we wear the badge which identifies us as sons of God. The Spirit has stamped life with a new nobleness – invested it with a moral and spiritual virtue which distinguishes it as the possession of Christ.

The arms which once were carried in proud opposition to God are now converted to His use. Beneath His banner we now fight, going into battle with the war-cry, "The world for Christ, and Christ for the world," fired with the dominant ambition to extend the frontiers of this Kingdom Church, and hasten the hour when all shall bow the knee and acknowledge Him as Lord of all.

Blessed, holy thraldom that makes me a prisoner to purity, a captive of the Cross; that brings me into eternal alliance with Him Himself; that strips me of my self-sufficiency, and casts me wholly

43

upon the exhaustless One.

> *Love delights the slave to be*
> *Of Him who died upon the Tree;*
> *We loved Him then at Calvary;*
> *We love Him now we do not see,*
> *And shall through all eternity.*

Of Francis of Assisi it is recorded that he was "a lover of God." This accounted for the glowing zeal, the undying devotion, and the unwearying service which glorified his whole life. Thus we see that the authority which Christ exerts and establishes over the life He has redeemed is that of love. In one of Dr. Stuart Holden's books reference is made to a character, "a self-willed girl, whose life had become enriched and beautified by a pure love. In explanation of the power which her hero possessed over her, she said, *'Well, you see, I love him, and so he can do anything he likes with me.'"* Is this not a faint likeness of that higher and holier bondage which our heavenly Hero and Lover has brought us into? His great love demands utmost surrender; and perfect love casts out all fear; all reserve is taken out of the response which we give; our abandon to His will is perfect and complete. Love delights to renounce its liberty, and yield to the law which governs its life. This life is only possible to those who know the reign of love – the fetters of obedience would prove irksome and painful to the spirit of any but those whose wills have been yielded entirely to God. The pathway would be far too difficult for other feet. True spiritual conquest can only be realised by those who are prepared to submit to this love-thraldom.

How little we realise all that this supreme servitude to the Divine would accomplish in us and make possible through us. Ignatius Loyola once cried, "Give me twelve men wholly surrendered to God, and I will convert the world with them." Somewhat extravagant words to use, and yet containing a great truth. The possibilities of life utterly God-possessed are tremendous – in fact they are only limited by the will of God. What God can do with life which He controls is occasionally seen in the ministry of those who have thus yielded. For example, "Hudson Taylor, one Sunday morning, whilst walking along the seashore at Brighton, heard the inner voice, which he knew so well, say to him: 'Hudson Taylor, I am going to evangelise Inland China, and if you will walk with Me, I will do it through you.'" What God wrought through this consecrated channel forms one of the most thrilling stories of missionary achievement in modern times.

Like others who have willed themselves unreservedly and irrevocably to God, Hudson Taylor proved how much the Divine hand can accomplish in one life and ministry.

Let us never forget that if we give ourselves to God in this wholehearted manner, God gives Himself back to us in fullest measure. It is only as we let ourselves go – literally throw ourselves upon God's will – that He can meet us in floodtide fulness; and only thus and then Can we prove the exhilarating and exultant joy of being utterly lost in God – carried captive in the Spirit to the heights and depths of Divine impartation and impregnation. As long as we so tenaciously cling to our own tiny resources, so long shall we remain but ankle-deep in spiritual experience. So many are content to wade, when God's plan is that we should swim.

> *Yes, all is mine; I'll use it all,*
> *The grand, the fair, the soft, the strong,*
> *To nerve my force for His blest thrall*
> *To whom I, having all, belong.*

O Master and Lover Divine, take possession of this vessel of fragile clay, filling it with the unpriced treasures of Thy grace and love. Let my whole life be transfigured and transformed by Thy indwelling glory. Make every outlet of my being a means of outpouring to the thirsting and tempted that lie all around my path. Take and till my heart, until it is prepared to be sown with the choice seeds of the Spirit – make it bring forth plentifully, yielding a harvest that shall fully satisfy Thee. Impress upon the softened and sensitive film of my soul the image of Thyself. Let it be like inwrought gold, deep and indelible, that will outlive the passing years, remaining untarnished and unfading.

Blessed Hope and Home of my life, lead me into more of the sweet mysteries of Love's dominion. Thou who art the central Source of heavenly fire, so unite me with Thyself that life shall burn with urquenchable flame. Break forth within me in fresh fountains of praise. Carry me beyond "the strange and tangled maze" of my own reasonings, to the shoreless deep of Thine own Word and will. Hide me in the pavilion of Thy presence. Keep me as the apple of Thine eye. Let me walk in the undimmed light of Thy countenance. Let me but know the joy

> *To follow, knowing not the way;*
> *If Thou shalt call, to answer, Yea!*

The Focused Life

If it be the pathway of pain that leads me into closer union with Thyself, then strengthen me lest my flesh fail, and I miss the best. Let me not refuse the cup because of its bitterness, neither shrink from the baptism because it means loneliness and loss. Help me, O Master Divine! that I fail not in the hour of crisis – lest I turn back from the steeps of Golgotha. Bid me come at all cost. Let me not crave a thornless, bloodless way – a path that misses the glory of Gethsemane. But enable me to give myself unsparingly to that perfect thought of Thine. In poverty cause me to know Thy wealth; in heaviness let me draw from the wellspring of Thy consolation; in temptation and test give me to partake of Thy stedfastness. Give me the wing of love-created desire, that I may follow Thee into the highest reaches of communion; woo me until my feet become like hind's feet in the path of consecration. Let me taste of the sweets of vicarious love – love that suffers yet sings – love that blesses even while it bleeds – love that will go down into woe's abyss with its Beloved – love that starts not back on the brink of calamity or catastrophe – love that counts it all joy to be found outside the camp with Thee. When Thy Cross is the heaviest, and the arrows of the enemy fall thickest around Thee, then let me press the closer to Thee – in that moment let me prove my allegiance and my love – let me glory in the fellowship of Thy grief.

O break my heart; but break it as a field
Is by the plough up-broken for the corn:
O break it as the buds, by green leaf sealed,
Are, to unloose the golden blossom, torn:
Love would I offer unto Love's Great Master,
Set free the odour, break the alabaster.

Sweet is God's will, whate'er it be,
To those who've opened eyes to see
That all which He permits is best,
For those who've found in Him their rest.
Who seek His glory first always
Shall prove His faithfulness all days.

THE SON'S DELIGHT

My meat is to do the will of Him that sent Me,
and to finish His work. – John iv. 34.

HERE we have the central source of the inspiration of the life of the Lord Jesus Christ, the underlying motive of all His ministry. The key-note of the music of that wondrous life is found in those revealing words spoken amid the travail of Gethsemane – "Nevertheless, not My will, but Thine be done."

Because Christ so completely gave Himself up to become the prisoner of the will of the Father, His life was large with spiritual content; He lived and moved in the environment of eternity; His inner spirit life was not confinable in the narrow orbit of the earthly. He was constantly removing life's emphasis from the natural to the spiritual – from the temporal to the eternal – from the earthly to the heavenly. His Kingdom was spiritual; His weapons were spiritual; His methods were spiritual. He directed the aspiration and ambition of His disciples toward a heavenly goal. All who came under His influence gravitated towards the same centre as Himself. He drew them upward, heavenward, throneward.

From these words of the Master we gather that He was possessed of a holy absorption – captivated and conquered by a supreme force which moved Him onwards to the fulfilment of all the Divine plan and purpose. He was not to be switched off from the main line of the Father's will by the calls or cares of the flesh. "Wist ye not that I must be about My Father's business?" are words that reveal the constraining impulse of His life. Higher and stronger than the claims of kindred was the call of His God-given ministry. Upon this vital constraint everything hinged and hung.

May we not learn from this magnificent utterance of our Lord that the will of God is always possible. So many place an exagger-

49

ated emphasis upon the frailty of the flesh, the helplessness of the human. And this is advanced as an excuse for laying down the will of God when it involves a cross. But if the words of Jesus Christ mean anything, surely they mean that not only is the Divine will possible, but that in the measure it is accepted or rejected, life is more or less strengthened or weakened thereby. To miss the will of God means an attenuated, emasculated Christian life.

> *Thy precious will, O conq'ring Saviour,*
> *Doth now embrace and compass me;*
> *All discords hushed, my peace a river,*
> *My soul, a prisoned bird set free.*

The circumstances surrounding this word of the Lord are not without their spiritual significance. Christ had just been engaged in the conquest of a soul – the wayside well had been suddenly tranformed into a penitent's form – and now comes the diverting appeal of His disciples – prompted doubtless by desire for the Master's well-being. Are there not often at hand those insistent counter-calls that seek to annul the holy passion for the highest and best? Those clamant, competitive influences that vie with the soul's truest and deepest consecration – those subtle, insinuating voices that penetrate right to the precincts of the sanctuary, and at times find their way to our consciousness at the very moment when we stand at the altar of sacrifice, ready to plunge the knife into that which threatens to stand between our soul and God? Those solicitous whispers of the flesh that bid us stay our hand, and choose some less thorn-strewn path.

The appeal more often than not is along the line of the lawful. Save yourself to-day in preparation for tomorrow; husband your strength – economise in the expenditure of your time, your vitality. The suave voice of the natural says, "Extravagance now will mean exhaustion later; take things easily; go more slowly; spare yourself!" We do well to remember that no loss can result from diligent and devoted application of all the powers of the being to the execution of the Divine will.

And does not the doing of the Divine will include the incarnation of God's thought – the translation of that thought into terms of everyday living? So that we might render the text that heads this article thus, "My meat is *to be* all that the Father hath planned; to lay bare to the world the heart and mind of the eternal God; to make known His infinite power; to declare His ineffable glory." To what a high level this lifts all Christian life; what a grand conception it gives of all service for Christ, where there can be nothing that is not sacred, since all is dedicated to this splendid end.

To His disciples our Lord said, "Whosoever shall do the will of My Father which is in heaven, the same is My brother, and sister, and mother"; thus teaching that whilst obedience may not determine relationship to Christ, yet the latter is revealed thereby. It is the same truth expressed in other words which we find in the tenth chapter of John's Gospel, where Christ said, "My sheep hear My voice, and I know them, and they follow Me". More often than not, action and attitude disclose character.

The will of God, great and glorious as it is, may often find its truest expression in our lives in the humblest form of service, such as on the surface may seem insignificant. To spend so much time in quest of *one* soul, and that soul, to boot, a Samaritan woman of unchaste character, when crowds were needing the light, appeared almost a wastage of precious energies. And yet, bear in mind, the saving of that one soul represented the will of God. It was part of the plan which the God-Man came to execute. Too often we focus upon statistics, we tabulate results, and we make our misleading calculations and comparisons; forgetting that sometimes the capture of a solitary soul may open the door to a mighty ingathering. How many times in the history of religious awakenings this has happened. The stream of revival that was destined to flood multitudes of barren lives, had its source in the surrender of one soul. The decision of young Spurgeon for Christ was a step fraught with tremendous consequences for thousands of souls who were to be won for God through his wonderful ministry. Sychar opened its heart to Christ through the medium of this woman's witness. And so we see that sometimes gigantic things may hinge on the devoted doing of that which seems relatively tiny and trivial. Because it involves the Divine will, to the earnest, obedient soul, nothing must be missed – small as it appears, yet its importance lies in the fact that it is a link in the chain of God's eternal purpose.

It is noteworthy that the Master employed words that indicate the Gospel in an active mood. His life-stimulus and sustenance were found, not in talking about the Divine will, not in thinking of it, nor in writing about it, nor even in singing of it; but in the *doing* thereof lay the Divine dynamic. A robust Christian life is never built upon emotions and feelings, it is in the realm of the will that the issues of life are decided. When the human will is anchored to and blended with the Divine will, then the whole life is redeemed from indefiniteness and vacillation. Think of the tremendous driving force developed when this union of the two wills takes place. It generates an almost irresistible power that makes Christian life victorious and virtuous, enabling the believer to prove the verity of the apostle's words: "God . . . that is able to do exceeding abundantly above all that we ask or think, *according to the power that worketh in us*."

How true and beautifully expressed are the thoughts of one in this connection who writes: "The will of God is as the force of a rushing river; to sail with it is strength, to strive against it, weakness. To do His work . . . that is not what He requires of us; His will is our duty. What is the work we do? To give a morsel of bread to a starving child? One word of His, and thousands can be fed with a few barley loaves and two small fishes. To nurse a sick fellow-creature? He does but speak, and the dead are raised to life. God does not want our work, but He does want our will. When we give it, we give all: when we withhold it, we give nothing."

Strive not so much to do, but learn to be,
That God himself may do His will through thee.
Better it is for thee to please him so,
Than by such ceaseless running to and fro
On errands which thine own blind heart hath planned;
Better to lay in His thy restless hand,
And let Him choose thy task, or keep it there
Inactive if He will: to do or bear,
His choice is best; I know in His great plan
That God can find a part for every man.

At the back of the man who utterly and unreservedly trusts God are all the measureless, exhaustless, fathomless resources of Omnipotence. The unfailing faithfulness of Jehovah guarantees triumph – God holds Himself responsible for such a soul.

THE TRIUMPH OF TRUST

Through faith . . . became . . . resistless in battle.
Hebrews xi. 33, 34 (A. S. Way).

THESE warriors of God were trained in the school of faith. They were ofttimes heavily handicapped and overwhelmingly outnumbered, yet always triumphant. They possessed a dynamic which levelled legions to the dust of defeat, and swept swarming armies of opponents into humiliating flight. Theirs was the path of the conqueror – they marched from "victory unto victory" – none could withstand their resistless faith. The experience of these Old Testament victors finds its counterpart in the lives of those New Testament warriors of whom Paul writes in his second Corinthian Epistle, "Thanks be unto God, which always causeth us to triumph in Christ." Or as another translation of the same passage runs, "Wherever I go, thank God, He makes my life a constant pageant of triumph in Christ."

They believed God, and so overcame. The secret of their strength was not in the subtlety of their strategy, nor in the prowess of their arms. "Not by might, nor by power" won they the victor's laurels.

We also, as followers of Christ, are called to soldiership. We must also grip the sword of service, and gird ourselves for the fray. 'Tis true we wrestle not against flesh and blood, but our enemies are none the less deadly, and the warfare none the less real. The weapons we wield are not carnal. We go clad in the Spirit's might, and armed with the sword of truth. C. H. Spurgeon once said that "the man who lives in the region of faith dwells in the realm of miracles." "Faith," he adds, "trades in marvels, and her merchandise is with wonders."

Faith will work the miracle
As we trust God's Oracle;

The Focused Life

*The victory of Calvary
Comes not through earthly strategy.*

What is there to hinder the twentieth-century warrior of Christ winning his way through all hell's opposing legions? Strong in the strength of the Eternal Spirit we may overthrow the adversary. The Cross is our answer to every thrust of Satan. We triumph in that precious blood victory of Calvary – in company with our Emmanuel we beat back the forces of darkness and disease – they are scattered before the battle-cry of an undimmed and undying faith in God. We draw our strength and courage from our all-sufficient and all-victorious Leader and Lord – it is the consciousness of our union with Him that inspires us to enterprise and exploit. In Psalm forty-six we find a wonderful "therefore" that couples us on to the Almighty. The Psalmist opens his anthem with the bracing reflection – "God is our refuge and strength, a very present help in trouble; *therefore* will not we fear." He surveys all the formidable host that are ranged in battle against them, and then having measured the strength of these things, he can still sing his enheartening song of utmost confidence in Jehovah.

A survey of missionary history during the past one hundred and fifty years will provide us with many a striking example of heroic and triumphant faith. When we read of the early days of the Bechuana mission, for ten long years no gleam of light seemed to pierce the prevailing darkness. "The Batlaping had open ears only to what promised temporal gains, and were deaf to all spiritual invitation or warning." When the sorely tried faith of the missionaries almost gave way, there was a holy woman in the mission who never faltered in her faith. She believed in the promise of the unchanging God, and she said: "We may not live to see it, but, as surely as tomorrow's sun will rise, the awakening will come." When her friends at home would have counselled her to give up her forlorn hope and go to a promising field, and when someone wrote her from England, asking what could be sent her that would be of use – the sublime answer of Mary Moffatt was: "Send us a communion service; it will be wanted." What mighty faith in the midst of such hopeless conditions! Yet when that communion service arrived on the mission field, three years later, it was at once put into use, and no less than one hundred and twenty born-again converts sat down to the Lord's Table. Thus God always honours and rewards faith.

This is undoubtedly a faithless age, when men believe nothing deeply, profoundly. Faith is shallow and shifty. We have, sad to say, passed out beyond the old days when men were willing if needs be to shed their blood rather than sacrifice their faith. The splendid, the

56

sublime thing about these people referred to in our text was their unstaggering confidence in the invisible God. And because of this they knew no defeat. Their faith makes them outstanding in the annals of the past; they are distinguished from the general character of the period in which they lived; their vision of God threw them out of alignment with the spirit of hollow ceremonialism which ofttimes surrounded them. They lived above the belittling spirit that whirled around them.

Says Archbishop Leighton, "God lays hold of us through our laying hold of Him." Thus God puts His omnipotence at our command for the accomplishment of His purpose, and for the overthrow of His enemies. He awakens within us such desperate desire that we become possessed by a victorious vehemence, that takes the kingdom by force; that refuses denial; that cuts its way through to triumph.

On the grave of Dr. F. B. Meyer may be found these significant words, "Here lies a man who reckoned on God." What a magnificent witness to a life lived in and for God. Mazzini, the great Italian, said, "Believe, and you will conquer." How true this is of those whose trust is in the living God. Somewhere else we read that "faith is not belief in spite of evidence, but life in scorn of consequence." Blessed Master, grant me grace to believe Thy Word in all its wondrous fulness, to take its promises in all their measureless meaning, and apply them to each and every need of mine! Make me bold to claim the fulfilment of that which Thy love covenants! Constrain my thirsty spirit to plunge deeply into the infinite and exhaustless ocean of Thy grace! Clothe me with that mighty, quenchless, unconquerable faith, that levels the mountains of difficulty to a plain, and puts me in possession of all the magnificent territory of Canaan! Teach me to bring each truant thought under the sovereign sway of Thy blest Spirit.

Thou art able, glorious Saviour!
Oh the rapture of the thought!
Shall we find it hard to trust Thee
Where all life with love is fraught?
Thou, whose love is never sleeping,
For the sweetness of Thy help,
Can we praise Thee as we ought?

O Word of the living God that searcheth the hidden depths of the human heart, bring to pass within this life of mine all that Omnipotent Love hath planned. Let me yield myself unto Thee even as Isaac surrendered himself to the sacrificial knife, that on "surrender's tide" I may be borne out to the place of enlargement, where I may desire more of Thine exceeding abundant goodness and grace. What if Thou shouldst choose to train me in the school of adversity, or take me to the throne of power via the cypress way? What is that to thee, O soul of mine? Hast thou not pledged thyself to the Lord for ever? Art thou not bound to thy King by "love's strong cord"? The furnace shall prove to thee the faithfulness of thy Beloved, and in the crucible thou shalt learn more of His consolations. The flames shall only strengthen the bands that bind me to Him – and even in the wilderness His voice shall be heard speaking *comfortably* to my heart. Shew me, O Lord and Lover of my soul, that it is in Thy wounds alone that I may wash away all that dims my vision, and drowns Thy call to conquest – that if I would pass through the portals of deathlessness it must be in intimate union with the blood-crowned Christ. Lift the veil, O glorious Nazarene, and bid mine eyes behold the noontide of victory – victory over all that dares to challenge Thy Lordship – let me see the illimitable horizon of a love-slain, and love-won universe – of a creation in harmony with its Creator – of a kingdom which swallows up and supersedes all other dominion – where all things are new, and the former things are passed away – a world whose remotest bounds know the sound of jubilee – where righteousness reigns supreme.

There shall be a performance of those things,
O trusting heart, the Lord to thee hath told;
Let Faith and Hope arise, and plume their wings,
And soar towards the sunrise clouds of gold:
The portals of the rosy dawn swing wide,
Revealing joys the darkening night did hide.

Sow on in faith! The Master knoweth all
The untried path, the ever-constant call
To sacrifice and toil. He trod that way;
He holds thy hand, and leadeth day by day.

Nay, He forgetteth not His servant's toil,
The seed so faithfully sown, on upturned soil;
The thorns and briars are thick, the "wild" vine grows,
And oft the promised bud the weeds disclose.

Sow on in faith! Thy "sheaves" thou, too, shalt bring,
And offer them with joy to Christ thy King;
Then, thy task ended, and the race well run,
How sweet will be the Master's voice, "Well done!"

GOD QUALIFIED MINISTRY

My qualifications come from God.
II Corinthians iii. 5 (Moffatt).

THIS is not, as easily might be imagined, the boastful expression of spiritual pride. Paul was not inflated with success, or carried away with a sense of spiritual superiority. It is the humble acknowledgment of utter dependence upon God, combined with a desire to shew that all the authority comes from and belongs to Him alone.

Has the apostle power to suffer persecution and privation? Is he able to withstand temptation, and overcome opposition? Can he look martyrdom in the face without flinching? Is he equal to the opprobrium of the Cross in every shape and form? Then it is because his confidence is in the Eternal God, and his source of strength alone in Him. His resources are not natural, nor his weapons carnal. He claims no credit for the conquests which mark his ministry, or for the unveilings of Divine truth which can be traced throughout his teaching. It is all of God! It is a river of power and glory which rises in God, and flows back to Him again. The Word which he preaches contains the authority of the throne – it is God-breathed. Those visible manifestations of the indwelling Divine energy are the proofs of his union with the Omnipotent One.

Is the apostle called to the vocation of a soldier? Then all his equipment is gathered from the Divine armoury. He fights with no carnal weapons against spiritual wickedness in high places – he marches against the ramparts of evil with no less trusty weapon than the sword of truth – he shields himself with no "enticing words of men's wisdom," but sallies forth to the fray under cover of the conquering shield of faith.

Or, to change the figure, is he chosen as a master builder in eternal things? Is he entrusted with the work of laying the foundation of the Christian Church? Then pay heed to the tools with which he labours, and the methods which he employs. Says Paul, "Other foundation can no man lay than that which is laid." How careful he is to see that the building is firmly established upon revelation – he does not erect his edifice upon the sand of tradition. "Thus saith the Lord" may always be found upholding the superstructure which comes into existence as a result of his ministry.

And so we too may surrender ourselves to the leading and working of the Holy Spirit, so that life becomes charged with a similar dynamic, and entrusted with a kindred authority. Our credentials may also have the seal of sovereignty, so that in the discharge of that divinely chosen ministry to which God's hand has constrained, we may claim the irresistible anointing of love and power – power to face all and fear none; power to do all that God commands, and be all that God appoints; power triumphantly to cleave our way through the thousand and one things that threateningly throng our path, to the goal of completion and perfection which the Lord sets before us.

Think it not strange if unbelief challenges the validity of your vision, and seeks to put fear into your heart. Stand strong in the confidence that you are chosen and called of God, and that consequently you are sufficient in Him for every God-ordained ministry.

Not men's degrees,
But bended knees,
To qualify for ministry;
The Lord of love, the Holy Dove,
Sends credentials from above.

To-day, we fear, the emphasis is on education – men make their boast in their intellectual equipment, and in their scholastic qualifications, glorying in their super-intelligence. They essay to combat the spiritual power of evil with weapons utterly insufficient for such conflict. "Not by might, nor by power," are these citadels captured, but by the power of the eternal and omnipotent Spirit – that Spirit whose wisdom is greater than that supplied by the most renowned centres of learning. He can bestow authority before which demons will "fear and fly."

He can confer credentials which will make ministry unmistakably Divine, and put the humblest preacher of the Gospel in the apostolic succession. Oh for more of that endued proclamation of the heavenly evangel! Teach me, O triumphant Christ, to tarry for power ere I go forward to any service for Thee! Give to my heart this vital assurance, this strengthening conviction, that "all my qualifications are from Thee!" Let me not lean upon the arm of flesh, nor look to the broken reed of my own understanding!

The remarkable change which took place in Wesley when at Oxford, through the anointing of the Holy Spirit, which he then received, is described thus: "His preaching was once like the firing of an arrow, all the speed and force thereof depending on the strength of his arm in bending the bow. Now it was like the firing of a rifle-bullet, the whole force depending on the powder, and needing only a finger-touch to let it off." What an example of the change which the advent of the Holy Ghost makes in a ministry.

Instance after instance might be gathered from the annals of sacred history, demonstrating beyond dispute how vital is this qualifying anointing from on high – this immersion which makes the weak things capable of confounding the mighty, and charges the "things that are not" with a remarkable power to bring to naught the "things that are."

Some glorious morn – but when? Ah, who shall say?
The steepest mountain will become a plain,
And the parched land be satisfied with rain.
The gates of brass all broken; iron bars,
Transfigured, form a ladder to the stars.
Rough places plain, and crooked ways all straight
For him who with a patient heart can wait.
These things shall be on God's appointed day:
It may not be to-morrow – yet it may.

TESTING BEFORE RESTING

There He proved them. – Exodus xv. 25

Yet he who hath never a conflict, hath never a victor's palm,
And only the toilers know the sweetness of rest and calm.

AFTER the triumphant deliverance at the Red Sea came the wilderness, and the bitter waters of Marah. This was part of Jehovah's permissive plan to put His chosen people to the test. The forbidding desert pathway is the way to the Promised Land – God has never promised His people to pass into victory via a rose-strewn path – to ascend the heights of glory 'mid the hosannas of earth.

We notice that the experience of miracle has its aftermath in the life of the Lord's children. Many are bitterly disappointed, and often much discouraged when they discover, after a wonderful time of personal outpouring, a season of severe sifting and searching follows. This is a necessary discipline. The test of Marah is preparatory to the rest of Elim. Soul suffering is the prelude to the sweetest spiritual song. It is all part of the soul's education and equipment.

It is the branch that bears the fruit,
That feels the knife,
To prune it for a larger growth,
A fuller life.

One saint of God once said, "The power of the Gospel is such that nothing can overwhelm, nothing embitter." And here we learn the sweetness of the Cross. The tree Moses cast into Marah's bitter waters to sweeten them is a picture of the Cross. It is in our hour of acute anguish of soul and spirit, when we tread some trackless wilderness way, or when we tarry by some Marah of humiliation or limitation that we discover the power of the Cross to bring relief – to soothe – to sweeten – to sanctify. The Via Dolorosa path becomes luminous with the glory of Calvary. No disappointment, no harsh treatment, no unkindness from other Christians, no pain, no infirmity, no continually complaining fellow-worker – nothing can poison the sweet waters of fellowship with the Risen One. His presence counteracts the sharp sting that otherwise would make the heart to bleed and ache.

> *O blows that smite! O hurts that pierce*
> *This shrinking heart of mine!*
> *What are ye but the Master's tools*
> *Forming a work Divine?*

With unutterable gladness we remember that Calvary is God's healing answer to all the world's want and woe. The deliverance from Egypt is a picture of salvation from bondage, but in the wilderness we are brought up against the *actual* in life. Every life has its central thirst to be quenched, and generally the soul seeks in the bitter, brackish waters of the world to find relief, till it learns of the Cross. The new-born soul must be put to the test. Its moral forces must be strengthened, its muscles developed by healthy effort. It must be taught the Divine sufficiency – it must prove the strength and skill of the Divine arm – it must learn to look to God alone for grace and guidance.

A recent publication called *The Ifs of History* conjectures what would have happened to England supposing Harold had won the Battle of Hastings, or to the world if Napoleon had won at Waterloo.

Supposing the Israelites had not stood the test, and had gone back once more to Egypt and slavery! Can we picture the world without the chosen people, without the Divine Law, and without the race that was specially prepared to cradle the Saviour of the world? Yet such is the similar loss to the soul that, having tasted the joys of salvation, anon tastes the bitter waters of the wilderness, is offended, and turns back into Egypt.

All healing of spirit, soul and body depends upon obedience. "If ye will keep My laws." Healing is not a changing of God's laws, it is the outcome of obedience. Obedience makes way for the manifestation of Divine power and provision. We cannot reach Elim, with its refreshing wells and palm trees, but by the pathway of surrender. To the yielded soul there is a glorious oasis in the desert, but to the rebellious and disobedient there is naught but a mocking mirage. Though the journey may be a difficult one, and though life is often a series of experiences of disillusion, yet our Guide will take us safely through all the travail and test.

In the realm of mechanics all machinery must be submitted to searching test. Iron and steel are tested and marked with their bending and breaking strength. Motors are taken trial trips on long and difficult hills. They must be proved fit for service or be thrown on the scrap heap as useless. We are apt to forget that God has saved us for a very definite purpose – that He wants those He can appoint to the great plan of His kingdom here on earth. We are saved to serve, though many Christians seem to think they are saved merely to have a good time. Some of our smaller country roads in England furnish us with a picture of the easy-going Christian. To the motorist these winding roads are a source of annoyance – a menace to his safety – a check upon his speed. One wonders at first why these roads twist and turn just when one wants to get up speed they never seem to go straight to a place. Then one realises they follow the bend of some river, or wander round the bottom of some hill; they are taking the line of least resistance, like some people who always take so long to reach their objective because they take the easy path. After awhile, with a breath of relief, one comes on to an old Roman road straight as a die, and then one can, with freedom and without fear, pull out and let go. The Romans possessed both military and legislative genius – they went straight to their objective. If a hill got in the way they went over it straight on. This is the antithesis of the line of least resistance; here we have dauntless determination, commanding courage. And so from the old Romans we may learn many a valuable lesson. When we come up against our mountains of hindrance let us go fearlessly forward. We must beware of the temptation to make a detour. The stiff ascent will be rewarded by the added strength and the new and extended horizon which we shall command at the summit.

Paul reminds us, in a page of his personal experience, that God tested him ere He entrusted him with the Gospel. Not as a novice did the great Apostle launch out into his missionary ministry, but as one who had been deeply taught and trained in the school of the Spirit – one upon whom the hand of the Lord had rested.

We sometimes contemplate admiringly the heroic in others. We covet their endurance; we long for their fortitude; we pray for their courage. But have we considered the price of power! How true it is that –

> *Heroes are forged on anvils hot with pain,*
> *And splendid courage comes but with the test.*
> *Some natures ripen and some natures bloom*
> *Only on blood-wet soil, some souls prove great*
> *Only in moments dark with death and doom.*

Each Marah holds some gracious meaning and ministry for the trustful heart. Many a soul can point to some place of special test and say, "There the Lord proved me" – some Peniel of fierce conflict – some Horeb of grave crisis – some Carmel of desperate need. Elim's cool and inviting waters were hidden from view at that time – but God led on until the heart-thirst was quenched.

O Thou who marchest on Thy triumphant course, leading multitudes captive in Thy train, I thank Thee that Thou hast not passed me by – that Thou didst not leave me in the far country, the prisoner of my own wilful ways. I bless Thee that Thou didst bring me to Thy banqueting chamber, and provide a place at Thy table for the prodigal. I thank Thee for the princely fare set before me – I who am not worthy to take the place of one of Thy hired servants – I who was bankrupt, bruised and bound – who dared not look for aught but judgment. Thou hast crowned me with loving kindness, and filled my cup with tender mercy. Thou hast anointed my head with oil, and caused my heart to overflow. Thou hast taken the broken vessel and shaped it afresh – out of the hopeless disorder bringing forth a thing of beauty, rich in likeness to Thyself. Thou hast made my soul to sing within me at the plenitude of Thy wonders which Thou hast wrought in my deliverance. Thou hast covered me in my hour of nakedness, and turned my arctic estate into a land that is filled with the glow of Thy love. Thou hast taught me that –

> *Satisfaction, full and deepening,*
> *Fills the soul, and lights the eye,*
> *When the heart has trusted Jesus*
> *All its need to satisfy.*

Here is God's loving challenge to you and me today. He wants us to think of the deepest, highest, worthiest desire and longing of our hearts; something which perhaps was our desire for ourselves or for someone dear to us, yet which has been so long unfulfilled that we have looked upon it only as a lost desire, that which might have been, but now cannot be; and so have given up hope of seeing it fulfilled in this life.

That thing, if it is in line with what we know to be His expressed will, God intends to do for us, even if we know that it is of such utter impossibility that we only laugh at the absurdity of anyone's supposing it could ever now come to pass. That thing God intends to do for us, if we will let Him.

LIMITLESS BUT LIMITED

He cannot prove false to Himself.
II Timothy ii. 13 (Weymouth).

It is well to remember that even God has bound Himself by His Word. The promise that bears His Divine seal cannot be broken – it must surely come to pass when those conditions by which it is governed are obeyed. God's faithfulness is assured – there can be no possible departure or deviation from that which the mouth of the Lord hath spoken. The apprehension of this fact will change our experience from a mere succession of religious moods and emotions into an established and unmovable attitude Godward and manward.

Just as the planets are kept in their courses by the unerring and unfailing power of the sun's sovereignty, so the promises of God are always assured to the believer by the changeless character of Him who gave them birth. God has no second thoughts – His first thought is His last. The Divine Word is eternal in its value and virtue. The ages roll on in tireless procession, but the God-breathed *Logos* remains unchanged and unchangeable. Like the eternal hills, whose majestic heads have soared heavenward in stately glory through the ages, so the Word of truth survives all the storms that have hurled themselves against it.

What a foundation upon which to rest! Here we may build a spiritual edifice against which the gates of hell shall not prevail – a temple that will not tremble at the blast of the terrible one. Upon this splendid assurance we may found an experience which will yield unspeakable blessing.

This is a law that governs in the kingdom of God – not merely that God can but that God *must* perform those things that He has promised. He cannot escape His own authoritative and inviolable Word – the Word spoken from all eternity – it is as stedfast as His throne.

He will perform the appointed thing and there shall be a performance of that which He hath said. We cannot conceive of the sun ceasing to shine, or the moon discontinuing his daily vigil over the sleeping earth. Then why should we stagger at the word spoken from above? Is anything too hard for the Lord? Dare we discredit the revelation of God in Christ? Shall we allow blindness to rob us of the comfort and cheer of these "exceeding great and precious promises," all of which are "yea and amen in Christ Jesus"? Do not overlook the fact that "nothing lies beyond the reach of prayer except that which lies outside the will of God." If it is part of the Divine plan, then faith may advance its claim to possession.

Limited by word and promise
To our little needs and care;
Limitless in love and power
All for him whose faith will dare.

Says Paul in writing to the Romans, "Let us be very sure that God is ever true to His Word." This blessed assurance is the soul's great and sure anchorage in every crisis and calamity of life. The man who thus accepts the inspired Word as God's binding pledge of performance shall never lose heart amid the conflict, even when the tide of battle seems to be going against him. This strengthening conviction shall nerve him to stand unflinching and unyielding in the face of the fiercest opposition. Surely no greater guarantee can be possessed by mortal than the Spirit-breathed revelation of Jehovah. He who clothes himself in this assurance is fortified against every possible emergency, and stands equipped with armour that no hellish missile can penetrate. To be weak at this point must ultimately prove fatal. God is prepared to furnish the trusting heart with ample opportunities of experiencing the faithfulness of His precious Word. And doubtless it will be chiefly in the fire of chastisement that we shall learn the deepest lessons of God's eternal veracity. He will permit us to graduate in the school of affliction in order that we may discover that naught His promise can annul. With this glorious conviction enthroned within, the believer is able to magnify His Lord when literally bombarded by the threats of the enemy; within the soul this priceless knowledge gives unceasing and increasing rest and gladness.

Think of the rich experience of some of those heroes of faith, who have risked everything in one glorious venture of trust in God. Take George Muller as an example of this – that long life, so full of remarkable proofs of Divine faithfulness. His life work represents what is almost a unique achievement. Think of it! A million and a quarter in answer to prayer! It is recorded of this modern apostle of faith that on one occasion he was asked by an admiring friend if he had ever doubted. "Yes, once," was his reply "I doubted for five minutes." It was this same saintly soul who said, "The beginning of anxiety is the end of faith, and the beginning of faith is the end of anxiety."

And then a review of the life of Hudson Taylor furnishes us with a further example of how fully God meets the man who dares to launch out in uttermost dependence upon Him. The thousands of souls which have been won for Christ from the heart of China provide an eloquent commentary on our text, proving that "God cannot say no to anything which He has promised."

Sometimes to step out on the Divine promise seems like courting disaster – to all appearance there is nothing but the void to walk upon. And yet to those who have learnt to tread the pathway of faith, life is brimful of victorious experience. Again and again, at the end of what looks like a cul-de-sac, stands Jehovah, waiting to usher us into some new domain of the Spirit – ready to teach us something more of the "exceeding greatness" of His power.

Dear tried and tempted soul whose heart has almost lost hope, let this inspiring word ring its silvery chimes through thy being. Listen to the sweet spiritual symphony which it bears to thy sinking soul – "He *cannot* prove false to Himself," and therefore cannot prove false to thee. Thou art on a Rock that cannot be moved.

Simon's response to Christ's command indicates the soul's victorious mood – "Nevertheless at Thy word I will." Blessed attitude of heart that keeps me ready for any heaven-given call; that makes me willing to face any frowning fortune that may confront me; that enables me cheerfully to accept any cross that love appoints. "At Thy word I will!" This is my unalterable answer to Thy command – the only answer that becomes a subject in the presence of his Sovereign. Thy word is sufficient reason for attempting the impossible and tackling the insuperable. Behind Thy word is eternal energy! Instinct with omnipotence, it cannot fail!

It is faith of this type that makes way for the miraculous in Christian ministry – that makes the desert into an arena wherein God may make bare His mighty arm. Though my action brings me into direct issue with precedent, and throws down the gauntlet of battle to prevailing opinion, yet none of these things need move me to alarm, since His Word is the authority for the position which I take. Let me but lean my whole weight upon that Word, and all will be well – after the noise of battle has subsided, I shall stand unshaken and unmoved. God cannot break His blood-sealed covenant with His people.

The Focused Life

O God of all power, bid me come to Thee, over the intervening waters – cause me to step out beyond the narrow bounds that fleshly wisdom sets. If Thy might is to find its manifestation in me then I must be ready if needs be to forsake the place of traditional safety, and throw myself upon the "seeming void." If Thou art to do the "new thing" within me, then I cannot tarry longer in my selfish security – I must be prepared to risk something – to loose my moorings, and seek a deeper anchorage in Thyself – a stedfast anchorage that shall hold me in the season of tempest and test, making me strong to resist the currents that would carry me far from Thee. Give me to –

Believe and trust: through stars and suns,
Through life and death, through soul and sense
His wise, paternal purpose runs:
The darkness of His providence
Is starlit with Divine intents.

There is a joy – all other joys exceeding –
A quiet joy, which time can ne'er destroy;
A joy through tears, through pain, through sore heart-
bleeding;
Thy joy is God – God my exceeding Joy.

When bitter words have reached me with their stinging –
Words base, unworthy, undeserved, and wrong,
God my exceeding Joy within up-springing,
My heart through Him hath still its music song.

THE MINISTRY OF GLADNESS

If you come . . . bring God's sunlight in your
face. – Romans xii. 8 (A. S. Way)

THIS is a ministry to which all God's people are called – a covering of glory which should adorn every service rendered. No office too great, and none too lowly for the exercise of this holy calling. The humblest, lowliest lot may be glorified by the heavenly sheen of gladness. Spiritual sunshine is all too rare in these days, and needs careful cultivation. The joy of the Lord will redeem life from tepidity and tameness, making it exhilarating and exultant. What a world of difference sunshine makes to a picture, lifting it from the commonplace to the sublime. The sunbeam falling upon the green sward transforms it into a golden glory, saving it from that palling flatness.

Faces that are bathed in the Divine sunlight are always beautiful, and usually supply a real tonic to those who behold them. Here is a veil of loveliness that may hide any natural uncomeliness.

And where shall we gather this golden glow? Where is the secret place in which we may generate this wholesome brightness? Is it not alone with God? – perhaps upon our faces, where no human eye can see. Here it is that God spreads His mantle of beauty over our waiting lives, removing the wrinkles of care and the furrows which haunting anxiety has ploughed over our faces.

Are there not those who come to us like ministering spirits, bringing in their train the very gladness of God? – shedding abroad that precious yet mysterious fragrance which comforts those who are cast down, restoring the drooping energies of the war-worn spirit, reviving the spent forces of faith and hope, rekindling love's declining fires. They touch us into newness of life – their genial, generous gladness is contagious. We find ourselves caught in the deep, strong stream of their joy – almost ere we are aware, our harps are off the willows, and song is rippling over the lips like some musical cascade. In such fellowship we find healing for the hidden wounds of the heart, and poisoned springs of thought and desire are purged by this pure tide of Spirit-born praise.

One writer, dealing with the subject of service, says, "The most serviceable gift which any man can give to the world is a radiant and inwardly victorious personality." And who but the Divine Spirit can baptise us into this life of laughter? Who apart from Him can anoint our lives with the oil of triumphant joy? Who can flood the deeps of our being with this abounding gladness but the Holy Ghost?

Charles Kingsley, writing on one occasion to his wife, said, "I wonder if there is so much laughter in any other home in England as in ours." Here was a home rich in radiant gladness – brimful of healthy mirth and merriment. What a false impression we may give to the world of our religion – we may drape it in mourning, give it the appearance of melancholy, instead of decking it with the garlands of gladness. Would that we recognised that God has called His people to tread the pathway of praise!

Of a dear disciple of Jesus Miss Amy Wilson-Carmichael writes, " She is always singing something. Her life is all sprinkled with songs."

Of Francis Xavier it was said by one of his contemporaries, "Sometimes it happened that if any of the brethren were sad, the way they took to become happy was to go and look at him." Francis of Assisi, we are told, "made happiness as much a rule of his order as poverty and obedience." Of the Franciscan movement in its early stages we learn that "the secret of its irresistible appeal lay in its spontaneous joy."

> *As we gaze on Jesus,*
> *So like Him we grow,*
> *To radiate joy and gladness*
> *With life-giving glow.*

Once more let us ask, What is the secret of this joy-robed, laughter-girt life? Is it but for a few choice souls, whose intimacy with heaven and heavenly things makes their garments smell of myrrh and frankincense? Has some inner circle of saints a monopoly of this holy resplendence? I trust not, for surely to all the redeemed comes the command to abound in thanksgiving. Is it not by turning our eyes upon Jesus that life becomes the vehicle of Divine lustre? To those whose vision is full of Him it shall be given to conquer gloom and depression – believers of this type shall interpret God in terms that will charm and conquer other lives.

Of Henry Drummond it is told how "he once went out alone into the high Alps. It was in the early morning. The stupendous heights encompassed him on every side. He was awed by their majesty – his soul bowed in reverent worship. And then he broke out into loud exuberant laughter." Overcome with the glory of Creation's splendour, the feelings of this man of God simply overflowed in the form of irrepressible joy.

Have we not at times realised this glorious experience, when it has seemed as though God had unsealed the springs of gladness within, so that rivers of praise burst forth and our whole being was deluged and drenched with "the joy of the Lord"? Under this baptism of blessedness all life was transfigured into radiant holiness and loveliness.

"Rivers," not a babbling brook, or a streamlet; not even a river, but " rivers." What Divine prodigality! In this experience, "Grace, not in rills, but in cataracts rolls." If it means anything, it means that there is no limit to the blessing God can send, through the feeblest of His servants, if they are prepared to receive what He is ready to bestow. Spirit-filled believers carry life, and satisfaction, and gladness wherever they go. Their presence is life-giving, fructifying, refreshing, even as a river which blesses as it flows.

THOMAS COOK.

FROM SPRING TO OCEAN

A well of water springing up. – John iv. 14.
Rivers of living water. – John vii. 38.
Life more abundantly (wave upon wave, the tidal onflow)
John x. 10.

Blessed, blessed ocean fulness
Of the untold love of God,
Reaching where no eye can follow,
And no foot hath ever trod.
Floating, sinking, carried on thee,
Let me prove His boundless grace;
Lying there in peace unbroken,
Gazing in His blessed face.

S HE had only come for a thimbleful, and he for just a sip of living waters. They had dropped in to a great evangelist's meeting, and from his overflowing cup they just tasted and went away. They could not have explained why they went. Perhaps it was that the coming of love had brought too a reviving of the religious instinct. "I only want you," she said, but she did want God's blessing on their joy. He only knew that love in his heart had awakened a strange yearning to worship. But the Word says, "He giveth not the Spirit by measure" – not in thimblefuls, and not in mere sips.

The taste left its hunger behind, and they went again, this time with a feeling that all was not well with them. Once more they listened and they heard of a woman, a sinful woman too, who was offered a "well within," that she might never thirst again. Their thirst was intensified – they must have this source of supply within themselves, and leaving their sins at the foot of the Cross, they found their emptiness filled from this living spring. How sweet and glorious life became! How wonderful everything was! What new meaning nature held! How radiant their little world suddenly seemed! Their love was lifted on to a higher plane. Their union was blessed by consecration to His service. The coming of the Divine enriched and ennobled all their human relationships.

Now they would be satisfied. They settled down to drawing water from the wells of salvation; preaching, witnessing, happy, but finding something lacking in their work. It was just the effectual that was missing. What could be the matter? Souls came to them for help, but though they seemed met in a measure through their ministry, yet they did not get landed on the Lord in out-and-out abandonment.

And then one day he picked up a book, the very title of which thrilled him – *Fulness of Power* – and he read, not of a well, but of a river. Again it was to be within, and was to gush out to thirsty souls. It was just the answer to their conscious need – just what met their longing souls. Together they sought that blessed Baptism that comes when Jesus is glorified. The well had overflowed – the stream had become a river, gushing out to and for others. All life seemed lit with new meaning, capacities were discovered and developed, prayer became a passion – the Bible a mine of wealth – the Lord an intense reality – they seemed to live in the supernatural. Together they laboured in the mission field; souls were being saved, the Cross was lifted up, and life was full of intense work. There were worse dangers too. Many were the foul streams and vile overflows from others that threatened the purity of their river. Sometimes when they saw the stagnant pools they wondered where truth and purity were to be found. They did not realise at the time how much they owed to the fact that their stream was flowing for others, nor how much they owed to not revelling in their own spiritual blessings.

One day she came to him exclaiming, "This work is utterly glorious – but!" "Yes," he said, "I'm not satisfied; we are so taken up with seeking and meeting souls; and nothing makes me so happy but – I am hungry myself. There is a wistful something within me unsatisfied." They both realised a powerful urge to seek something deeper, fuller, richer in God. They worked, the work grew, claims multiplied to such an extent that at last they were almost invalided home for a rest. Completely exhausted, they longed to get to the quiet hills alone with the Lord. But they must needs go to a convention first.

The evangelist was there – it was good to meet him. It called to mind their first filling. The author of *Fulness of Power* was there, and they had many a wonderful talk, but somehow they were not met, they were not satisfied.

No one seemed to take much notice of the stranger. He was so quiet, so unobtrusive, so retiring, but somehow there was such a deep settled peace in his face; from his eyes shone the light of a wondrous inward glory. They were drawn the moment they saw him.

Just a few quiet words, and they knew he could shew them–he could open the door to their hearts' deep need. Away up on the hills they read "Satisfied" – how it thrilled them! Their friend had brought them past the rushing rivers, and to their astonished view, before them lay the mighty ocean, the boundless, shoreless deep. They quietly entered on its bosom; it was the ocean of Divine Love. Another Baptism in which all tiny cups get filled and drowned, to which all wells and sources finally should come, and in which rivers great and small lose themselves. It was Himself who is Love – who came that they might have life more abundantly. It was the tidal onflow, wave upon wave; their own little fulness was forgotten! They had entered His. No longer were they occupied with the fringe of things – they seemed to have entered right into the holiest of all – the gifts and the works which hitherto had held them so tenaciously now gave place to the great Giver and Worker Himself. That one thought became central and supreme – Himself. With the first flush of dawn the winged desire of love rose to Him. A new sense of union with Christ possessed the soul. A wonderful life of worship commenced – from within them welled up a ceaseless fount of love, praise, and adoration. They had now learnt the secret of worship – He was satisfied in them, and they were satisfied in Him. All service was transformed into a sacrament, from which rose the incense of adoring love. To them "to live was Christ," all things became possible – suffering was a delight. There was such a sweet sense of the enfolding, enveloping Presence. The Cross possessed a new and wondrous significance and charm. Through them from Him flowed the power which stilled the storm of anxious care. They could now sing with deep, sweet meaning –

Covered, covered by the ocean,
"Buried" there and out of sight,
"Raised with Him" in glorious union,
Walking in unclouded light.
Ever brightening is the pathway,
Ever deepening is the flood,
Covering the "earthen vessel"
In the glory of its God.

On their return to the mission field they were astonished to find how hungry were the born-again souls. They had not realised before how strong was the need. And now their work became deeper – there was a satisfiedness in the heart of the One whose soul-travail had been that His own should be conformed to His image. The waters no longer spread shallowly but went deeply – there was brought forth that depth of character that tells. They were no longer the centre of admiring crowds. Though the people came more and more, they were no longer "marvellous workers," for they were "lost" in the Divine ocean. People no longer clung to them for help, for as soon as they came, their eyes were attracted as by a magnet to the One they were gazing upon. They no longer touched the glory which now all belonged to Him. They ceased to covet, praise, or strive to win the reputation of successful workers.

Nor was there any feverish overwork, or painful friction. The quiet peaceful will of God was done. There was no strain on the personality. A wondrous stillness reigned within. When terrible cases of demon possession, etc., had to be dealt with they were at once switched on to the All-powerful One. They were so lost in the ocean of Divine love that personal attempts to draw them failed. The secret of their successful ministry was not in them – they did not attract, it was the Lord who drew. The Cross had snapped the chains of self, and they were free, gloriously free. Now every act of daily life however simple was significant to the kingdom of God. The smallest ministry was the channel through which some of the fulness flowed.

Thus "step by step," stage by stage, the hand of the Lord had led them up the steeps of desire, down into the depths of trials, on and on until at last they found themselves swallowed up in the Infinite – lost in the Eternal – wrapt in the glory of the Omnipotent.

SATISFIED

Once I tasted, 'twas from others,
Little sips of living water;
Heard a voice among my brothers
Calling to a thirsty daughter,
Till my weary soul drank deep
From the source where sinners weep.
As I yielded in my spirit
Came the spring itself to rise.
Carefully I tended, watched it,
Till it grew in depth and size.
Just a tiny stream there trickled
Down the hillside of my life;
Thirsty wanderers stooped to drink it,
Fresh and sweet, and free from strife.

From Spring to Ocean

Gradually it grew and widened
Then the boats and ships came by.
Glad was I that God could use me,
But 'twas not without a sigh;
Still I thirsted for completeness,
Did not understand my cry,
Till the ocean burst upon me,
And I lost myself thereby.
Lost my little stream within it,
Lost my mighty river too;
I have found Divine completeness,
Now I know what He can do:
On the bosom of the ocean
Pour the radiant rays above,
Draw the water back to heaven,
So my soul is drawn by love.

A vessel may be half empty, or full, or overflowing. It may be the source of a stream to fill others as Elisha's widow's oil. But put the vessel into the sea. It is full; yes, soon it is overflowing; yes, and more too – it sinks to the bottom lost in the ocean.

At first it is so often our own little fulness of which we are so conscious; but later it is all lost in His Fulness. We become gloriously conscious of the ocean of Divine love.

LOVE'S MIRACLES

Is there some problem in your life to solve,
Some passage seeming full of mystery?
God knows who brings the hidden things to light;
He keeps the key.

Is there some door closed by the Father's hand
Which widely opened you had hoped to see?
Trust God and wait – for when He shuts the door
He keeps the key.

Is there some earnest prayer unanswered yet,
Or answered not as you had thought 'twould be?
God will make clear His purpose by-and-by;
He keeps the key.

Unfailing comfort, sweet and blessed rest
To know of every door He keeps the key,
That He at last when just He sees 'tis best,
Will give it thee.

PREFACE TO THE FIRST EDITION

THIS is the third volume of heart-to-heart talks which we have been constrained to send forth, the last two volumes having already fulfilled a most helpful ministry to many of those who crave for a closer union and communion with their Divine Lord and Lover.

In these days of spiritual declension no need is greater than that the believer possess an experimental knowledge of that holy anointing which comes from close contact with the Risen Lord. The spiritual strength which is generated in the "upper room" of fellowship, proves an invaluable equipment in the season of suffering, in the hour of humiliation, or in the time of testing. Without this we are weak in the face of the foe and unable to sustain the conflict.

We trust that these pages may yield some comfort, bring some blessing, and vouchsafe some inspiration to those whose feet tread the "solitary way," and who go down into deep waters with and for their Lord. The writer desires no greater guerdon for his labour than this.

E. C. W. B.
June 1931

Love is the mighty master-passion, the irresistible power of attraction, the omnipotent driving energy of the kingdom of God, and this tremendous and transforming love-possession is only made possible and actual by the indwelling of the Holy Ghost.

E.C.W.B.

LOVE'S MIRACLES

So then these abide unperishing – Faith, Hope, Love . . . but chiefest of these is Love. – I Cor. xiii. 13 (A. S. Way).

Oh, how skilful grows the hand
That obeyeth love's command.

HENRY DRUMMOND wrote his immortal work on love, choosing as the title of this spiritual and literary gem, *The Greatest thing in the World*. We are in complete agreement with the writer when he thus ascribes to love the sovereign place among the fruits of the Spirit. "And now abideth faith, hope, love, but the greatest of these is love." Who can deny love this place of preeminence and predominance, seeing that it has been responsible for some of the greatest achievements of the ages? When other forces have failed, and fled from the field vanquished, the power of love has swept everything before it in its triumphant advance. The might of the sword has been compelled to bow to Love's omnipotent sceptre – the bitterness of man has shrivelled up beneath the burning rays of this victorious virtue – the puny arm of prejudice has been paralysed in the presence of this resistless love-tide. Faith has moved its mountains and wrought its wonders, but love has exceeded and excelled faith in its mighty works. Faith has conquered its thousands, but love has slain its tens of thousands.

In all the armoury of God no weapon has proved more effective than this Damascene blade of love. It breaks through the most stubborn defence, melting adamant conditions.

We remember reading the parable of the Sun and the Wind, both claiming to be the stronger. In their effort to establish their respective claims to superior strength they endeavour to make a woodman remove his coat. "I will blow my coldest and hardest," said the Wind, but the woodman only drew his garment closer round him. "I will pour my warm rays down upon him," said the Sun, and lo, what the cold blasts failed to accomplish, the Sun did. It is so with love.

> *Tho' I have all other graces,*
> *Tho' I speak with tongues aflame,*
> *Tho' I sit in heavenly places,*
> *Tho' I magnify Thy Name;*
> *I am but as brass resounding,*
> *Nothing in Thy sight I prove;*
> *Till thro' faith, by grace abounding,*
> *I am perfected in love.*

Love's fire can consume the stubble of bigotry. Look at Saul of Tarsus, the proud and intolerant Pharisee, bent on the extermination of the Christian Church – invested with religious and legal authority he sets out on his merciless and murderous errand, eager to apprehend those defenceless disciples of Christ. But the Lord of Love meets him en route for Damascus. Love pierces all his defences, and with one stroke lays the haughty bigot broken and bleeding, submissive and surrendered, at the feet of Jesus. Saul has capitulated to a force against which even he is powerless. Love has wrested the throne of this life from the tyrant usurper – self. There he lies prostrate in the dust before the Lord. Listen to his language, "What wouldst Thou have me to do?" Love has done its work, and done it thoroughly. O Love, Thou art irresistible! What fortifications will not fall when Thou dost arise! Thou makest all men Thy slaves – none can withstand Thee!

> *O Love, that wilt not let me go,*
> *I rest my weary soul in Thee;*
> *I give Thee back the life I owe,*
> *That in Thine ocean depths its flow*
> *May richer, fuller be.*

If we look into the pages of the past two hundred years of missionary ministry we shall be amazed at the marvels wrought by Love. We shall discover heroism so splendid, so sublime, as to amount almost to the miraculous, and all and only made possible by love-clothed, love-anointed service. In some of these records we see Love conquering conditions that make the sensitive reader recoil with a shudder. We find Love voluntarily accepting the most repulsive environment – plunging into depths of defilement – going down into the dark shadows of hell to rescue and reclaim perishing souls. We behold Love stripping itself of the sweets of congenial society, burying itself in the heart of slumdom – emptying itself of the pleasures and joys of ordinary life. How true it is that "those Christians who have wrought most mightily to heal the wounds of the world have prevailed by virtue of their own mystical union with the Everlasting Lover and Redeemer of souls." It is always the love-inspired servant who renders the truest and most lasting service – whose ministry is dripping with the blood of self-sacrifice.

The perusal of a book like *God in the Slums*, or *Down in Water Street*, shows how some of the mightiest miracles are achieved down in the depths of the moral morass of the world's mighty metropolises. Or take Amy Carmichael's book, *Over-weights of Joy*, and see how "from India's coral strand love has claimed its priceless jewels."

Then we not only contemplate the miracles of ministry of these sent ones of God, but we think of some of the miraculous fruit which has resulted from their consecrated labours. Who can read the life of Pastor Hsi and not be thrilled through and through at such a transformed life, redeemed and revolutionised by Divine grace? – brought up out of the horrible pit of paganism in which he had been reared, and made into a new creation in Christ Jesus.

Think of the African whose life was redeemed by the grace of God from the grossest darkness and depravity. Picture the bloodthirsty Hottentot plundering and pillaging, leaving a trail of terror behind wherever he went, with a price set upon his head, but none daring to attempt his capture. And yet Love found a way into the heart of this poor benighted heathen. The grace of God came into his life, and changed the demon-possessed into a devoted disciple of Jesus Christ.

We are not indifferent to the amazing achievements of human ingenuity and intellect; the world is full of memorials to the genius of man, reminding us of those, though long since dead, whose skill gave many of those blessings which enrich twentieth century civilisation. And yet in no other realm can we discover such trophies and triumphs of supernatural power as in the kingdom whose law is love. The feet of Love have trod where other feet dare not tread – Love has shouldered burdens that would have crushed a lesser power – it has scaled inaccessible heights – extracted the poisonous and bitter sting of evil from many a life-wound – kindled fires that will burn for eternity.

This unutterable and unrivalled love can perform its miracles with material that is both unlikely and unusable. Love is not limited to lives rich in natural or intellectual endowment. It can take hold of the coarsest and commonest channels and transform them from within. It can apprehend its Mary Magdalenes, its John Bunyans, John Newtons, Richard Weavers, and its Billy Brays, and make of their lives radiant reflections of redeeming grace. "God takes the ordinary and makes it the vehicle of the Divine." Think, too, how Love can remould the vessel that was marred on the "wheels of life," shaping into beautiful and chaste design, fulfilling all His original purpose.

We must not forget that Love often works its greatest wonders and wins its noblest triumphs not in the arena of the spectacular or sensational. Quietly, gently it moves along its victorious pathway. Without ostentatious display it claims its conquests. Like the gradual incoming of some mighty tide, lifting upon its bosom a hundred heavy craft, so this wondrous love-force takes possession.

We think of the men and women who have laid themselves upon Love's altar for service in savagedom – who have gone forth at Love's command to almost certain death. We sing of their glorious prowess in jungle and desert – but what of the mothers who were willing to sacrifice their treasure in this way – who were willing to suffer the surrender of their dearest and best? They are often overlooked, and their part of the consecration lost sight of. Many a mother has gone back to her humble and lonely lot with much of the light gone out of the home through the departure of her only child, and yet she has not withheld her costly offering. At the feet of the Master she has broken her choice alabaster box of precious ointment. In a very real and deep sense she has been nailed to the cross. Is not such love wonderful and beautiful to behold? Are these not some of the hidden heroisms of which Love is the great first cause?

Think of the miracle of Love's patience. How God has waited through the long years for our answer to His call. When we read the inspired analysis of Love as contained in I Cor. xiii we are not surprised to discover love achieving such spiritual and moral miracles. "Love patiently persists, love is tender. Love is not envious, is not pompous, not ill-mannered, not irritable – makes no personal demands. Does not impute evil motives, has no taste for anything impure, but a responsive delight in all that is genuine. Love shelters all things, is always trustful, always sanguine, always composed. Love can never, at any time, lose its colour, nor fade away." (Translated from the original Greek by William Pitfield.)

> But "Love is the greatest of these!"
> Love is life to my soul;
> For it binds my spirit to God's,
> Who is "Love," and my goal.

In the next place let us observe that *love costs*. Immediately Love comes to birth in the life, that life at once becomes exposed to suffering and sacrifice. Into whatever relationship or realm Love enters it plants the standard of suffering and sacrificial service. Love works its miracles but only through the medium of Cross-filled lives.

A touching story comes to mind of "a maiden whose mother was very beautiful excepting her hands, which were shrunken and shrivelled and unsightly. For long, with the delicate reticence of girlhood, the little girl said nothing on the matter, but at last her curiosity overpowered her. 'Mother,' she said, 'I love your beautiful face, and I love your beautiful eyes and brow and neck, but I cannot love your hands, they are so ugly.' Then the mother told her the story of her hands. She said, 'when you were an infant, sleeping in your cradle, one night the cry of fire rang through the house. I rushed upstairs and found the nursery ablaze. But God led me right to your cradle, and I saved you. But ever since then my hands have been like this.' The little girl was silent for a moment and then she cried, 'Oh, I still love your face and eyes and brow, but I love your hands best of all.'" That mother's love cost her those beautiful hands – all her life she bore the marks of her devotion.

Then again, *love awakens*. Think of the soul to which is unveiled the wonder of the Divine Love as revealed in the Cross of Calvary. Life has been asleep – dead, but now under the transforming touch of this unfolding of the heart and character of God, it awakes and life becomes charged with a terrific and splendid meaning. How often this is seen in human life and love.

"A modern artist, dealing with this ever young and ever old theme of the awakening of the heart to love, represents a young woman sitting by the fire, the room lit only by its glow. In her hand she holds a letter which has awakened her to read aright the secret of her heart. Suddenly all things change for her. She thinks of this unaccountable glorifying of the common day. Happy she had not been. She had been most wretched. She had been blind and deaf. She was only half a woman . . . and 'I never saw that before,' she says aloud; 'I never saw a great many things before. I am amazed at the suddenness of my awaking. Love passed through this house to-day, this house that other people think is just the same dull place it was yesterday, but to me there is a splendour in every room.'"

Thus love transfigures, and amazes, and glorifies.

And after all what is the new birth but the awakening of the soul to love's true mystery and meaning? Is it not then that the soul's

vision is cleansed and clarified to discern the beauty and wonder of
life? Well might the pen of the poet seek to express the heart rapture
which possessed him in that radiant moment of soul birth:

> *Heaven above is softer blue,*
> *Earth around is sweeter green,*
> *Something lives in every hue*
> *Christless eyes have never seen.*

Who that has thus looked out upon life with the joy of salvation burning in his bosom but has felt a flood of glory break upon him
as he has viewed nature? Every blade of grass has been clothed with
a mystic charm – each woodland glade has shone with the winsome
wonder of a new creation – each unfolding flower seems possessed
with a deeper fragrance – every breeze comes laden with the message and the music of redemption – heaven and earth are pregnant
and vibrant with eternal meaning. The whole face of things has been
marvellously changed, so that the regenerated soul looks out upon
and lives in a new world. Love has lifted the veil and brought in the
light of an endless day.

> *Grandly rolling o'er the region*
> *Where was once but pain and woe,*
> *Are the waves of love's pure ocean,*
> *Which in ceaseless rapture flow.*

Then further, think of Love as the great life-dynamic. It holds
the two-fold power of drawing and driving those lives which come
within the radius of its influence.

In the ministry of soul-winning, unless we are *endynamited*
with love and the love that "patiently persists," we shall not see the
miracle of changed lives. In the fifteenth chapter of Luke, that chapter of inspired parable, we see in each instance the earnest quest for
that which was lost. We also find the sequel to the search in the re-
covery of that which had been lost. The Evangelist depicts that quenchless love of the Shepherd-Saviour in those significant words, "Until
He find it." How untiringly the search continues until the straying
sheep is safe in the shelter of the Shepherd's arms. In the third and
last parable we find the father going out to meet the repentant prodigal. Love had not lost heart. Love still stands expectant, and as the
curtain falls upon the scene, we witness love triumphant. Love has
finally driven the far country from the heart of the prodigal, and drawn
the prodigal from the far country, back to the homeland of forgive-

ness.

Many volumes might be filled with the stories of miracles wrought through the ministry of Divine Love. Some the miraculous character of which might easily be overlooked.

An open-air preacher was being severely heckled by able adversaries. "And what did Providence do for the martyr Stephen when he was being stoned to death?" was the jeering enquiry. A sudden prayer for help, and quickly came the Holy Ghost response – "God gave him grace to say, 'Lord, lay not this sin to their charge,' which was a greater miracle than sending twelve legions of angels to save his life." And it was.

We who gauge miracles so largely by the extraordinary do not always realise where the marvel lies. Stephen's ministry on earth was crowned with the greater miracle of love which probably broke the heart of the watching and listening Saul of Tarsus.

There was a young medical student who, after a hard day's work of professional study, had spent the evening teaching and managing a ragged school. A little fellow, shoeless, hatless, shirtless – with no home, no father, no mother, and no friends, begged for shelter. Hardly believing the boy, the student followed him to see his usual abode for the night. Climbing a wall they found eleven woebegone boys clad in their rags, sleeping in the gutters of the iron roof. That night in the heart of that student who had wanted to go as a missionary to China, Dr Barnardo's Homes was born.

And so Love's torrent dashes in its cleansing, healing course, coming from Calvary's open fount, reaching down to the poor bleeding, broken, sin-ridden world. Love was wounded for our transgressions, bruised for our iniquities, and by Love's stripes we are healed. Naught but Love – Love Omnipotent – could staunch the terrible sin-wounds of this prodigal planet. Calvary stands out as the greatest miracle of love that this world has witnessed – such unparalleled, incomparable love cannot but ultimately achieve its purpose in world-wide sovereignty.

Not until each loom is silent,
And the shuttles cease to fly,
Will God unroll the pattern
And explain the reason why
The dark threads are needful
In the Weaver's skilful hand,
As the threads of gold and silver
For the pattern which He planned.

LOVE'S ALTERNATIVE

But if not . . . ! – Daniel iii. 18.

Somewhere, for God is good,
Life's blossoms, unfulfilled,
Must spring from dust and gloom
To perfect bloom.

WHAT is the root motive underlying our acceptance of the Cross? Is it the hope of reward – the prospect of some princely recognition from the Divine hand? Is it the expectation of deliverance that holds us to the uninspiring and uninviting path? What if there is no promise of reward – no hope of deliverance? Wilt thou still press on and face the frowning future? If God sees fit to keep you in the fire – to prolong the period of painful persecution – of fruitless toil – of misunderstood ministry. What then? Will thy faith fail? Canst thou utter this doughty challenge to all that seek to turn thy feet from the Calvary track?

We need some shadow o'er our bliss.
Lest we forget the Giver;
So, often in our deepest joy
There comes a solemn quiver.

"But if not . . . !" This is the language of irrevocable choice – of unalterable allegiance; the cost has been counted, the Cross embraced, because it represents the will of God. Faith staggers not at the furnace-filled future. The thorn-pierced experience leads to a place on the throne. It indicates uttermost submission to the plan of God. A God-begotten courage and carelessness that defies intimidation and withstands *intolerance*. "Do thy worst, O haughty tyrant. We prefer to die in obedience to the Divine will rather than live in disobedience to that will. If deliverance comes not, then be it known, O king, that it is not a question of Divine ability, but of Divine sovereignty. Are we not the possession of Jehovah, and shall not He do with His own as He will ? 'Tis not ours to dictate to the Almighty."

Perhaps 'tis along the line of delayed answer to prayer that the test comes. How desperately you have pleaded the promises and urged your need of the longed-for response to your petition.   But though the weeks have developed into months, and perhaps into years, since first you presented your plea, yet you are still waiting for God's fulfilment of your request. Others have asked and received. Why not you? Beloved, though thy heart thrills at the thought of realisation and possession, yet – *"if not?"* Can you bravely bare your breast to the keen edge of such a possibility? Will your lips still voice the glad refrain of complete consecration? The icy blast of bitter disappointment has been responsible for the withering of many a fair flower of grace – like the east wind it has chilled both faith and joy, nipping the tender shoots of holiness. It is only that soul who can utterly trust God that knows the triumph which robs disappointment of its bitterness.

> *If perfume in my soul there be*
> *That could to others comfort bring;*
> *Whate'er it takes to set it free,*
> *I'll suffer, Lord, and through it sing.*

Like your Master will you still respond with that victorious "Nevertheless"? Remember that although Peter was delivered from his dungeon in response to the cry of his brethren, yet Stephen was permitted to perish amid the hail of murderers' missiles which opened to him the gates of glory. Remember also that though it is recorded that some saints "escaped the edge of the sword" by faith, yet others "were tortured, not accepting deliverance." Satan will always devise some means of escape along the lines of compromise, but it is not ours to invite or evade suffering. To escape the anguish of this present time might mean irreparable loss. The fire will be God's means of softening, sweetening, and strengthening our Christian character, creating within us that exquisite response to every guiding gesture of the Holy Spirit. A celebrated teacher of singing, speaking of one of his most promising pupils, said: "Her mechanical execution is excellent, indeed it is almost perfect. She has full control of her voice, and knows all the outside of her art. But she lacks soul, and she will have to suffer before she can get it. If only something would break her heart she would be the greatest singer in Europe." It is just equally true of the spiritual life, it flows fullest where some great convulsion of sorrow has made a channel.

> *"God is His own interpreter" – such truth stands ever true;*
> *The Love His hand hath hid in darksome guise*
> *The deep, deep thoughts of God – the Only-wise*
> *God only can unveil the human eyes,*
> *God must explain Himself.*

Perhaps the way to victory in certain directions seems closed, and though you have sought diligently to move the obstacles which barred your path to your heart's desire, yet the barriers still remain. Do not let a single doubt fasten upon your mind to bring you into unrest and unbelief. Though the mountains still block thy way, and the waters are too deep to permit thee to pass over, give not way to fretful fear. Rest in the Lord – stay thyself upon him – keep step with the Holy Spirit. Leave this problem with God, it is too hard for you. He will work it out – He holds the solution to all – a solution that will surprise and gladden you in the day when His "rich purposes" are fulfilled. *"But if not . . .!"* Then God knows best.

In the school of God, we shall grow rich and strong through the discipline of difficulty. These are God's messengers and means of deepening our life in eternal things – of awakening within us a quicker response to His touch and a clear apprehension of His purpose.

> *He thwarted all*
> *My fairest schemes;*
> *Beyond recall*
> *Banished my dreams.*
>
> *Sadly resigned*
> *To bear His will,*
> *I thought to find*
> *Griefs sharper still*
>
> *But He in love*
> *No doubts could tire,*
> *Gave joy above*
> *My heart's desire.*

Job, the man whose experience made him familiar with the fire, could say, "Though He slay me, yet will I trust Him." And again, even when his path was veiled, he could sing, "When He hath tried me, I shall come forth as gold." Exactly the same spirit that possessed and prompted Shradrach, Meshach and Abednego. Perhaps in the eyes of others your position may appear paradoxical, and the question may be hurled at you, "Where is your God?" "What doest thou in such sorry plight?" These and other stinging taunts may be thrown at you by those who wish to wound and seek to dissuade you from this utmost union with the Cross. Let your answer be an unfaltering and unflinching attitude of confidence in God. Do not struggle to justify your position before men, but be careful to retain a right relationship Godward.

Hudson Taylor when passing through one of those great soul crises, wrote, "I seem to be writing from the inner chamber of the King of kings – surely this is holy ground. I am striving to write a few lines from the side of a couch on which my darling little Gracie lies dying . . . It was no vain or unintelligent act when, knowing the land, its people, and its climate, I laid my wife, and the darling children with myself on the altar for His service."

In one of those magnificent passages which we frequently find in the Minor Prophets, Habakkuk mounts up to a glorious altitude of triumph in God.

He says, "Although the fig tree shall not blossom, neither shall fruit be in the vines; the labour of the olive shall fail, and the fields shall yield no meat: the flock shall be cut off from the fold, and there shall be no herd in the stalls: Yet will I rejoice in the Lord, I will joy in the God of my salvation." How that victorious *yet* rings out in the midst of the night of adversity, sending its melodious chimes far out into the dark and ominous shadowland in which the prophet dwelt. Here is a joy that is independent of earthly environment – a song that is subject to no hellish force. This is the language of a soul that pierces the veil of the visible, and discerns God in all things. A soul who, possessing God, is content with anything and everything that He permits. Such a soul is not subject to loss – possessing nothing it enjoys all. Christ-centred and glued to God it walks scathless through the fiercest fire.

It is well to remember that at the back of all calamitous circumstances stands the throne of God, that He is the Great First Cause in the lives of those who acknowledge His Lordship. Nebuchadnezzar's power was limited; he could light the fires of martyrdom, but God could render the flames powerless! Let us not overlook the fact that deliverance *in* the fire is a greater miracle than deliverance *from* the fire.

Love's Alternative

Be still, my soul,
When through thy treasure-house devouring fire
Leaps hungrily, consuming vain desire with scorching breath.
Fear not the cleansing flame;
Be still, my soul, and call on God's great Name.

It is the uttermost surrender that results in uttermost satisfaction. And the soul can never realise real consecration without complete faith in God. Dr Steele gives a beautiful illustration of this. He says, "A glass-worker makes a beautiful yet exceedingly frail ornament, and brings it to his friend as a gift. He says, 'This is yours; it is very delicate, and must be touched with the greatest care.'"

"'But,' says the friend, whose hand has been outstretched for several minutes, 'why do you not let go your grasp and give it to me?'

"'Oh, because I am afraid that you will take hold of it so strongly as to break it, and all my labour will be lost,' replies the giver.

"'But you say it is mine; let it go, then, and if it is shattered in the transfer, the loss will be mine and not yours.'"

It is as we let ourselves go thus to God, regardless of the consequences, that we are made to prove the mountain-moving power of the Lord in deliverance. God works on the behalf of those who fear not to fling themselves upon the bosom of His faithfulness.

Patient, resigned and humble wills
Impregnably resist all ills.
My God will guide me by His light,
Give me victorious might:
No pang can me invade
Beneath His wings' propitious shade.

For the soul that gives itself away wholly to God, the Divine Hand always holds something incomparably better, and infinitely more precious, than anything we may be called upon to relinquish for His sake. God meets the abandoned heart with unpriced spiritual wealth such as none but those who leave the choice with Him can understand.

E.C.W.B.

SOME BETTER THING

God having provided some better thing for us
Hebrews xi. 40.

My wish for thee? "God's best!"
His love errs not, and none but He can choose aright;
Thy need, unknown to me, is clear in His pure sight, –
I would not place a limit by a finite wish of mine,
But this I pray,– that all thy need be met by Love Divine.

HOW absolutely adequate and ample is God's provision for the demands of His people. Not a single need but what has been abundantly anticipated. No unfilled gaps in that life which the Master moulds; no painful periods of spiritual penury; no seasons when the source of supply is sealed. The "good thing" is always available to those who leave the choice with Him.

And yet at times have we not acted as though we doubted the wisdom of His will? As though we feared the consequences of His choice? Preferring to walk in the dim light of "reason's glimmering ray" rather than trust His far-seeing love. And thus have we grieved the gracious Spirit who sought to bring into our lives some "better thing." How foolish for one moment to hesitate to accept that which His love arranges and appoints. How loth we are to lose those things, which, by reason of long possession, have acquired such a secure hold upon our affections. How the tendrils of the heart twine around the earthly treasures! We cling to them so tenaciously, failing to see that our Heavenly Father seeks not to impoverish but to enrich; not to deprive us of our joys but to add thereto; to increase the fruitbearing capacity of the branch which He now prunes.

Alas, in our blindness we covet that which counts for so little in the eternal sense, whilst we sacrifice that which would yield abiding blessing; influenced by selfish considerations we choose some "well-watered plain" which offers so much but really gives so little, and so we miss God's "better thing," the advent of which would transform our lives. Can we wonder that deep down in the heart disappointment reigns? That shadows of bitter regret hang over our sky, dimming its brightness? This must invariably be the outcome of a choice that is contrary to the Divine will. It is this unsurrendered selfhood which prevents God carrying to completion all His choice design.

But to you who mourn over failure to follow the guiding cloud of His presence, we would say, "Be of good cheer!" The future may still hold for you God's "better thing." Wait awhile at His feet and to your now humble, hungry heart shall come afresh that cleansing, comforting, captivating call which shall for ever end the inward unrest. Out of that unutterable longing of yours shall be born the sweet surprise of a new revelation of Divine glory.

Sometimes this "better thing" comes in the shape of an added cross, which threatens to crush us beneath its weight. Perchance 'tis the temporary eclipse of some special spiritual vision; the severance of some sacred association; the failure of some precious project; the sudden sealing of some secret spring of pleasure; the loss of some valued vocation; the withdrawal of some substantial temporal support. This is all in order to woo thee to the "better place."

Beware, beloved, lest at this point your soul succumbs to the severity of the test! Though this "better thing" appears at present such a "bitter thing," "sit still until thou know how the matter will fall." Judge not the Lord by feeble sense – a little more patience and you shall find that "this thing" is indeed of the Lord, and moreover is one of the "all things" destined to accomplish the Divine purpose in your life. Still those anxious fears! Cast thy care upon the Lord! This is His response to your repeated appeals! He is now at work in your life making room for the "better thing" which He is preparing for you. To-day's "dark enigmas" will end in "hallelujahs sweet." The sequel to thy suffering will be beyond thy highest expectations. A new energy and enthusiasm shall adorn thy days! The painful parenthesis shall pass, and leave thee amazed at what awaits thee.

The introduction of this "better thing" will mean so much to both God and man; the life of the sanctuary as well as the service-life will be all the stronger and sweeter. Greater results will accompany the ministry and a larger freedom will be enjoyed in worship. Dear reader, put to the proof this Divine promise! Let it become the spiritual stimulus of all thy actions! The compelling conviction of every attitude of heart and mind! The assurance of attainment in things Divine! Adoringly acknowledge His Mastership and Ownership, and this glorious "better thing" shall be your reward!

> *Better than my brightest thoughts shall be*
> *The full unfolding of Thy love to me.*

We turn to the world of nature and there we find this principle in operation. The glory of springtime is the gracious herald and harbinger of the imminent summer. The budding trees, and the myriads of dew-laden shoots which adorn each smiling bush, are all tokens of Nature's "better thing" which ere long will appear to glorify the countryside. It is creation's hour of awakening, when she throws off the sleep of winter – the earnest of each early spring song of the birds in their woodland aviaries foretells the coming of that greater and richer summer anthem which the feathered choir anon will sing amid the summer sunshine. These things are the promise and prophecy of that "flower-decked earth" which is to come. As in the natural, so in the spiritual, God ever leads His people out of the lesser into the greater, out of the morning into the meridian glory. And so it is that God graciously gives to His children these welcome earnests of that which is laid up in store for them. Even now the hand of God is laying the foundation of that "better thing" in our lives. God's ways are past finding out, and we can only stand in worshipping awe in the hour of rich fulfilment of His word, and cry out, "O the depth of the *riches both of the wisdom and knowledge* of God! How unsearchable are His judgments, and His ways past finding out!"

As we trace the outworking of the Divine plan in an unfailing providence, shaping our lives according to His eternal purpose, the soul is lost in wonder, love and praise. Out of the storm has been born the radiant rainbow of promise, encircling the dark clouds of circumstances, until they have shone with hope. We have learnt that God's thought for our lives is far better than our most cherished scheme.

Perhaps even now the Holy Spirit has spoken the earnest of that better and bigger thing – it is one of those secrets of the Lord that may not be uttered until the set time of His choice. Ruth little realised that God's hand held such a sweet surprise – as she gleaned day after day in the fields of Boaz there was little to forecast that dazzling future to which she was slowly but surely being led. It was a humble path to the possession of the prize, but God "finished the thing" so that the Moabitish maiden came to her own. The "better thing" was awaiting her at the termination of the time of testing. In due season we shall reap if we faint not. God may withhold the lesser in order that we may possess the greater.

To Abraham of old God came and breathed into the heart of

the patriarch the promise of the "better thing" to come, a child of promise – one who should be born for the accomplishment of the Divine purpose. The fulfilment of that hope was long delayed – the precious promise seemed to tarry. It was as though God had overlooked the word that He had spoken; as though the word of promise was destined to be buried amidst the accumulating years. Yet through those long years of waiting Abraham "staggered not through unbelief, but was strong in faith . . . believing that what God had promised He was able to perform." And then at the latter end of life, came God's "better thing" in the shape of a son – a God-given child – the outcome of the Divine will.

To the crushed and bleeding hearts of the disciples, Calvary could only be interpreted as a lamentable loss which involved their irremediable ruin. From whatever angle they viewed the Cross it spelt overwhelming failure. By no possible mental miracle could they conceive of the Cross as a triumph. And yet Golgotha was for them and for us God's "better thing."

Out of Israel's bitter bondage was born the "better thing" of gracious deliverance. Through the darkness they came into the more abundant light – their light affliction wrought in them a more exceeding and eternal weight of glory.

God says, "I will do better unto you than at your beginnings." What an encouragement for the future! Great and glorious as the past has been, yet such a promise speaks of a "yet to be" which shall entirely eclipse all that has gone before. The dawn may have had its splendours, but they were only forerunners of that "exceeding and eternal" glory which they heralded. All God's beginnings are the gracious earnest of magnificent completion – the stream that had its source in Jehovah shall also find its home in Him.

God is always making ready within us for the greater grander thing – preparing the way for the richer spiritual harvest. Do not hastily conclude that God has done His best at birth – that is merely the breaking of the day through the darkness of the night – that is but the faintest hint of the wondrous development which is to follow through the years. The unfolding of salvation's wondrous plan in its personal application shall go on throughout the timeless ages of eternity – the sun can never rise upon that day which sees the revelation of God exhausted or fully compassed by man. Always an "abundant" reserve for the soul that is pledged to press on in the Divine way.

Through the pages of inspired prophecy, poetry, and history we catch faint glimpses and glimmers of that new covenant glory which was to appear with the advent of Christ. To the Jewish ceremonialist the ritual of the Mosaic Covenant contained a glory which in his estimation could not be eclipsed – to him it was the highest altitude of revelation – the utmost limit of Divine unveiling. And so although the Prophet and Preacher alike predicted the advent of the new day of spiritual splendour and moral glory, yet their mind was sealed to the true meaning of that which their inspired lips uttered.

Is it not ofttimes a sad fact that the Church of Jesus Christ is more or less blind to the "better thing" which God desires to incorporate into her life and experience! It is the most difficult thing to arouse a people from this state of complacent contentment – to stimulate ambition for God's highest and best. Anything that disturbs the rest of orthodoxy is deeply resented, and regarded with hostility. And yet have not most of the remarkable manifestations of Divine power and glory been the result of intense desire for more of God? When the soul of the people becomes quickened into active quest for greater light and truth (the pulse of desire beats more powerfully) then it is that God's "better thing" appears. Men catch a glimpse of the new vision on the horizon of inspired Writ, and they become ardent seekers of its fulfilment in their lives – they weigh anchor and launch out from the harbour of self-complacency into the ocean of possibility in God. In the days of Martin Luther the Church saw God's "better thing" in the teaching of justification by faith. It stirred the slumbering saints in Zion; she arose in response to this truth, and shook off the trammels of popery and priestcraft.

It was so once more in that period of spiritual dearth and departure from the highway of holiness, which prevailed at the time of the Methodist awakening. These evangelicals arose to call the attention of the Church to the truth of sanctification by faith – the wells of practical godliness had been choked by the debris of tradition – the voice of the prophet broke upon the deadly stillness and stagnation, light commenced to break through the dark clouds – springs sprang up fresh and sweet, and a new thirst for God and eternal things was begotten. Men saw that the arm of the Lord was waiting to work a new thing in their midst – that the heavens were ready to overflow in copious and beneficent showers – that the hour of holy visitation had arrived. To compare the England of the early part of the eighteenth century with its spiritual condition fifty years later, reveals how the heavenly vision had wrought tremendous transformation in the religious life of the people – an altogether new conception of God and His claims had gripped the consciousness – many of the old and established abuses had disappeared. The compass of the Church shewed that the course had been completely altered. God's "better thing" had taken the place of the paralysed and impoverished state into which the Church had fallen.

109

Oh, the blessedness of being absolutely conquered! Of losing our own strength, and wisdom, and plans, and desires, and being where every atom of our nature is like placid Galilee under the omnipotent feet of Jesus.

The heart that serves and loves, and clings
Hears everywhere the rush of angel wings.

THE TRANSFIGURATION OF DESIRE

Thou openest Thine hand, and satisfiest the desires of every living thing. – Psalm civ. 28 (free translation).

He shall give thee thy heart's desire.– Psalm xxxvii. 4 (The Great Bible).

Though you may not know the reason,
Let not faith and patience tire;
In His own appointed season
God will grant your heart's desire.
It shall come in full completeness,
And your heart with joy shall brim;
They shall know an added sweetness
Who wait patiently for Him.

HEART'S desire! What a thrill runs through us as we picture the goal of our hopes! Perhaps we started life and service with tremendous energies and high hopes, and we have been disappointed of immediate success. We have come along a path where failure, disappointment and perhaps disillusion have taken the first fresh glow of zeal from our ministry, or from our life plans. We look back over the vista of the past, and seem to trace naught but thwarted plans and shattered dreams. We had stood on God's promises – we had trusted Him, and now it seems we may have misinterpreted or misunderstood His will for us. Then one day our cloud-obscured vision is pierced by a passage like this – "He will fulfil the desire of them that fear Him," or "What things soever ye desire, when ye pray, believe that ye receive them, and ye shall have them"; and from the depths of our being come a big response and a new throb of hope. It is as though God had dropped this healing word into the cup of our bitterness, to turn it into a spring of satisfaction. He whispers in the

111

depths of our spirit, "Even now thy lips shall taste the sweetness of My own fulfilment. Thou shalt discover the best wine at the latter end of the feast. I will do better for thee than at the beginning."

There is little doubt that to every true Christian such scriptures as the above have meant much deep heart-searching. It has led the soul to probe the depths of desire and ask, "Are my desires right ones? Are they the desires God means to fulfil? Where is the point of departure 'twixt His thought and mine?"

For those who are in real earnest there is a digging into the depths of the heart to try and ascertain the spring source of desire. And ofttimes it means a humbling unveiling of motive before the inner depths are reached, shewing what is the true foundation of desire. We must not overlook the fact that God confines His promise of fulfilled desire to those aspirations and ambitions which find their genesis and goal in Him. It is for us to yield ourselves so completely to Him, that He may work in us those desires that fit in with His plan.

> *I hunger and I thirst,*
> *O Christ, to be yoked to Thee.*
> *Break every barrier down.*
> *Exquisite unity!*

It is extraordinary how easily we may deceive ourselves, so that often desires rooted in self may be completely camouflaged by some "service" for God. For instance, desperate desire for success in Christian service, though it commands the admiration and commendation of the onlooker, may be nothing more than human ambition for self-advancement. The almost vehement effort to promote those projects which will result in self-gratification and glorification are indicative of the driving power of a subtle form of selfishness. This may or may not be evident to others, but the flesh resents the light of truth which would tend to strip off the veneer, and reveal things in their true character.

There is a tremendously strong current of desire within for the natural, normal human aims for happiness, reaching out after that which appears to be the needful goal. To one it may be the craving for power – to another the thirst for position – whilst to a third it is the longing for pleasure. There is no doubt that God means man to find full expression for all the capacities and talents with which He has endowed him, and as God is allowed to lead, there need be no fear that the life will not find that sphere of service in which those talents may find their fullest, greatest and most beneficent expression. There are so many splendid capacities that might be used in the service of

Christ which suffer from suppression – instead of being directed into right channels they are simply stifled. A false method of reaching the Divine ideal is largely responsible for this state of things.

It is true that in the intensity of our feelings and desires, we greatly differ from one another. It has been said that "intensity of life is a mark of the greatest men." Ruskin it was who described passion as "the most truly poetic or making force of all – and want of passion the truest death."

Intense desire means intense endeavour. If we trust God entirely and wait patiently, we shall find we must live on the altar, and when we have learnt to be weaned from earthly desires, He will see when we are fit to be trusted with His fulfilling.

This has been the experience of many a true Christian – intense longing has been laid upon the altar – intense endeavour has been generated. The soul has learnt that the intensest desire is for God, and has let go all other only to find that God has granted a new resurrection – they are now fit to be trusted. "I give Thee back all that Thou hast withheld," was the cry of a medieval saint who had learnt a deep meaning in the Cross – the glory of renunciation. Before the goal can be reached passion must learn patience, and few can be patient and wait – the Cross receives from them not a glad response, but a lifeless acquiescence to what may seem inevitable. Let there be a living response, not sulky submission. Let the strength and love and service that might have been for self, be poured out for Him and for others.

> *Transfigure the passion within me,*
> *Release the energy there;*
> *Let God's love in the depths of my being*
> *Be a love that others shall share.*

Frequently the temptation is to resort to purely natural means to bring about the fulfilment of God's promise, instead of quietly and believingly moving with God and waiting for God. The time element plays such an important part in our calculations, and consequently we become impetuous and impatient, whereas if we had the vision of God, we should be content to tarry for the Divine moment of performance and possession.

The Spirit-filled life invariably begins with intense hunger for God. It is the "earnest of the inheritance," and an entering into new desires for His perfect plan – for holiness and for service, and perhaps most of all for His coming – to behold His face, when He will put all wrong things right, and end the suffering of the world. God arouses this intense desire for Himself that the soul may follow hard after Him, through all difficulties to find full satisfaction in Him. At times the soul is keenly conscious of the limitations of the flesh, and the cry goes up to God,

> *My heart it pants for Thee,*
> *O burst these bonds and set it free!*

The Holy Spirit is given to the believer to energise for service. That *dunamis* that "works effectually" takes possession of the nature, and according to the strength of its desires – its intensity, its passion – so the Holy Spirit can use it. Desire is transfigured on to higher planes, and belted into sacrificial ministry.

This intense craving for God becomes the seed-plot out of which springs a precious harvest of noble action and achievement. The flame of desperate desire leaps upward to Him. The river of longing flows ever more swiftly and smoothly towards eternal things. The pursuit of the utmost fulness of and likeness to God becomes the absorbing quest of the being. The soul is consumed with desire to realise in fullest measure that purpose and plan which is "alive with love, and overleaps the last limit of what we ask or think." It is Watt who sings:

> *And every power find sweet employ.*

The conditions for fulfilment of our desires are very clear – it is the desire "of them that fear Him," and it is for those who "delight themselves in the Lord." A right apprehension of the Cross and its place in our lives is the key to the fulfilment of our heart's desire. There are many in the Christian life who preach "death to self," who are merely re-voicing the old medieval theme of holiness through the cloister. There is a mutilation of life which leads to all kinds of spiritual pride and unreality. Christ says, "Let him deny himself," and Paul, "I am crucified with Christ," but this does not mean the mutilation of life as practised by the ascetics of old, and by many a modern "saint." We are indeed to be dead to sin, but when we try to mutilate our human nature, we shall soon find ourselves on the stilts of the Pharisee. This only results in the misdirection and false application of desire. Thousands often unconsciously take the ascetic path, and miss the glory and joy of a life of full-orbed expression, which brings holier joys and a glorious consciousness of power. It has been said that those who are most truly spiritual are the most simple and natural, and surprisingly human. Spirituality means the vision of God in common things, and the manifestation of God in common tasks.

The Transfiguration of Desire

Christ says, "Take My yoke upon you," and it is in the acceptance of that yoke that life reaches its highest consummation, and therein finds its richest energies turned into channels of truest and most fruitful service. Oh, for a heart that knows only the sovereignty of God-breathed desire! That seeks and strives alone for that which it is His will to bestow! Life will then be replete with unspeakable blessedness.

> *Trust, hopefully trust,*
> *That God will adjust*
> *Thy tangled life: and from its dark concealings,*
> *Will bring His will, in all its bright revealings,*
> *Then trust, trust,*
> *Hopefully trust.*
> *For the glory and the passion of this midnight*

I praise Thy Name, I give Thee thanks, O Christ!
Thou that hast neither failed me nor forsaken
Through these hard hours with victory overpriced;
Now that I too of Thy passion have partaken,
For the world's sake – called, elected, sacrificed!

Thou wast alone through Thy redemption vigil;
Thy friends had fled;
The Angel at the Garden from Thee parted,
And Solitude instead
More than the scourge or cross, O Tender-hearted!
Under the crown of thorns bowed down Thy Head.

But I, amid the torture and the taunting
I have had Thee!
Thy hand was holding my hand fast and faster,
Thy voice was close to me;
And glorious eyes said, "Follow Me, Thy Master,
Smile, as I smile Thy faithfulness to see!"

SHUT IN

And the Lord shut him in. – Genesis vii. 16.

Shut in with Thee, O Lord, for ever,
My wayward feet no more to roam;
What pow'r from Thee my soul can sever?
The centre of God's will my home.

SHUT in! What a wealth of spiritual meaning these words convey to the illuminated and anointed mind. They at once suggest a life of close fellowship and conscious communion with God. How eager the Lord is to bring His people into this place of hallowed union with Himself. Too long have we lingered in the "outer court" of an impoverished experience, content with an occasional visit to the "inner sanctuary" where He is wont to reveal the Shekinah glory of His presence; satisfied with a temporary vision of His matchless beauty. Let God lead thee into the cloudless glory of this sacred spiritual enclosure.

For marvels of this sacred place are known
To him who in it dwells with Thee, alone.

If we consider the lives of some who have walked the pathway of loneliness and separation we shall then discover the value of the discipline of the shut-in place. Joseph's shut-in time as slave and prisoner was a time of preparation for fruitful service. Paul's three years in Arabia was evidently a time of revelation when God prepared him for his future ministry. Frances Ridley Havergal tells how through ill health she was shut in with God, and so often shut off from the outward ministry. She gives the beautiful explanation that there must be long learning before we are fit to teach others.

Love's Miracles

Learning long, before your teaching,
Listening long, before your preaching,
Suffering before you sing.

The experience of being "shut in" is as necessary to the Christian life as the rest of winter is to the tree. There are times when all outward ministry seems cut off, and the soul, perhaps through circumstances or sickness, is shut up to God. Winter is the time when all the sap of the tree is stored in trunk and roots as the great preparation for the spring budding. So, too, the winter of death and stripping is preparatory to the fresh up-springing of resurrection life.

Bishop Wilkinson says, "A life-long experience has taught me that at *very* important times some one who cares about the work has to be taken apart, not so much to pray as to suffer, to 'fill up that which is behind of the sufferings of our Lord.'"

There can be little doubt that all great revivals in the life of the Church and in the life of each of its members has been brought into being through and preceded by a shut-in experience.

Be still, and know He doeth all things well
Working the purpose of His holy will,
And if His high designs He do not tell
Till He accomplish them – do thou be still.

Why should'st thou strive and fret and fear and doubt
As if His way, being dark, must bode thee ill ?
If thine own way be clearly pointed out,
Leave Him to clear up His and be thou still.

From this "shut in" place we may wield the most precious and powerful influence in the Kingdom of God, and render the truest and most abiding service to the Church of Christ. Here it is that a spiritual passion, an irresistible inward impulse, will be generated that shall mantle our lives with a loveliness all Divine. Life shall be crowned with a deep restfulness and quietness – the continual chafe will be removed and the current of experience will flow evenly and steadily in the channel of the Divine purpose. A new spiritual rhythm will mark our movements when life's pivot is thus changed from self to God. The soul shall rise from the dust of defeat into a life that is vibrant with victory. In this place of holy converse with God thou shalt learn Jehovah's latest thought, and discover how thou mayest do God's work in His own way, and thus be spared the pain which the introduction of thy natural ideas and plans invariably brings. Thy life shall be made after "the pattern" of that inner and finer vision which comes to the soul when "alone with God." Here thou shalt acquire the power to sing:

> *One great eternal "Yes"*
> *To all that God shall say.*

Hitherto thy Christian life has been brimful of anxious activity, and the "shut in" experience is new and strange. But be of good courage! Fear not the silence of thy surroundings. Thou art in the school of the Spirit, there being trained for future service; take full advantage of these precious preparation days; they are pregnant with profound possibility. Make haste to acquire all the deep teaching which He will give. He will keep thee here until fully equipped for the next step in His perfect will. Do not chafe under the discipline or resist the restraint of the Holy Ghost – this will only cause delay. Remember He is moulding thee for eternity. He is bringing thy patience to perfection. Much depends upon thy attitude towards this particular phase of the Divine work in thy life. Much may be gained or lost at this juncture. Therefore watch and pray. Be obedient! Recognise that God is working "all things" for thy good. Be still!

> *As thou seekest fruit from the seed-planted grain,*
> *Seek life that is living, from life that is slain.*

God is wooing thee from thy idols; He loves thee and love is jealous over the object of its love and so He wants thee beautiful, "without spot or wrinkle." He hath brought thee up from thy wilderness wandering and want. Thou art now come to the place of banqueting and blessing. God hath brought thee home! Here He will speak to thy heart of things that could not be uttered or understood in the "outer court." God's hand is upon thee! He is performing the "appointed thing" in thee and perfecting that which concerneth thee. Seek not to escape from this blessed ambush which thy Lord hath set to capture thee. Allow thyself to be taken prisoner by Him who loves thee with everlasting love. All that is now taking place is but God's wonderful answer to thy deep heart need, and the prelude to that larger ministry for Him. When thou hast come forth from the fire, then thou shalt sing:

> *I'll bless the hand that guided,*
> *I'll bless the heart that plann'd.*

Love's Miracles

"The legend runs that there was a musical instrument upon which nobody could play in an old baronial castle. It was complicated in its mechanism; and during years of disuse the dust had gathered and clogged it; while the dampness and variations of temperature had robbed the strings of all tone. Various experts had tried to repair it, but without success; and when the hand of a player swept over the instrument it woke only harsh discords and unlovely sounds. But there came one day to the castle a man of another sort. He was the *maker* of the instrument and saw at once what was amiss, and what was needed to put it into repair. With great care and skill, he freed the wires of the encumbering dust, and adjusted those that were awry, and brought the jangling strings into tune; and then the hall rang with bursts of exquisite music." Thus God would deal with thee if thy life has become tuneless and discordant. In the "shut in" place He would remove that which makes for discord, and teach thee life's truest, sweetest harmony.

As thou dost linger in the sacred stillness of this happy trysting place thy garments shall smell of frankincense and myrrh, and thy clothing shall be wrought of gold. His arm shall encircle thee and draw thee down into the place of rest beneath the shadow of His wings. Here the things that puzzle and perplex, the things that sting and smart, shall be lost in the radiance of the Divine presence. Tears and turmoil shall be turned to tranquillity and triumph as we tarry in the "hollow of His hand." Satan hath purposed to sift thee as wheat, but God hath determined to ripen thee for the rapture. Thou art graduating for the glory of that hour when He shall call thee to meet Him in the air.

In this wonderful "shut in" place thy soul shall move on swiftly and smoothly in its appointed course; though ofttimes the circumference may be in a state of storm, at the centre peace shall prevail. That marvellous stream of resurrection life that flows from the Throne of God shall bear thee on its bosom to the goal that God hath set before thee and which hitherto hath appeared so inaccessible.

> Still and sweet the silence deep
> Where no foot hath ever trod;
> Softer than an infant's sleep
> Is my rest in God.

There are undercurrents in the ocean which act independently of the movements of the waters on the surface; far down too in its hidden depths there is a region where even though the storm be raging on the upper waves, perpetual calm and stillness reign.

120

So there may be an undercurrent beneath the surface movement of your life – there may dwell in the secret depths of your being the abiding peace of God, the repose of a holy mind, even though, all the while, the restless stir and commotion of worldly business may mark your outer history. Thus within the sacred inner places of the life reigns that undisturbed assurance of God's control – of God's prevision and provision – of the Father's all-sustaining grace.

If chosen souls could never be alone
In deep mid-silence, open-doored to God,
No greatness ever had been dreamed or done!

When we have exhausted our store of endurance,
When our strength has failed ere the day is half done,
When we reach the end of our hoarded resources,
Our Father's full giving is only begun.

His love has no limit, His grace has no measure,
His power no boundary known unto men;
For out of His infinite riches in Jesus
He giveth and giveth and giveth again.

ANNIE JOHNSON FLINT

POSSESSING OUR POSSESSIONS

Rise . . . up . . . and . . . commence to possess.
Deuteronomy ii. 24 (Spurrell).

> *Oh, for the breath of the Spirit,*
> *Oh, for the might of His sword,*
> *Leading us on to inherit*
> *All that in Jesus is stored.*

WHAT a stirring challenge to conquest! What a clarion call to claim our inheritance in God! Shall we respond to this inspired invitation to press forward to possession of the promised prize? Or shalt we let the challenge lie unheeded and unanswered?

The achievement of spiritual ambition is only possible to consecrated and concentrated endeavour. There can be no conquest without conflict – no advance without abandon. It is the voice of God seeking to provoke within us a holy aspiration to compass and conquer the land.

But alas, there are too many who linger in the land of limited possession. So much Christian heritage lies unclaimed in the chancery of unbelief. Spiritual poverty is more often than not the result of indolence or indifference. If we have sought it has been in such a half-hearted manner that naught but failure could possibly attend such lifeless, listless quest. There has been no fire in our utterance as we have come to the throne – no glowing passion in our souls as we have entered the courts of the Lord – no light of desperate desire in our eyes as we have approached the altar of intercession.

Now and then we hear of some bold, believing soul who reaches out after the unspeakable blessedness of Divine fulness – those who go up and claim their blood-purchased birthright. "Rise . . . up . . . and . . . commence to possess." Is there no answer within us to this glorious encouragement to conquest? No adequate response to this gracious invitation to enrichment? The possibility of possession should urge us forward. Dare we hesitate when such spiritual plenitude lies at our disposal? Let us give God a courageous and chivalrous answer to His sovereign summons – an answer that is worthy of those who fight beneath the standard of the Cross. "Being absolutely certain that whatever promise He is bound by, He is able also to make good" (Rom. iv. 21, Weymouth).

> *"Rise up! Possess!" Commands are strong,*
> *And nerve us to be stronger;*
> *He gives the strength, He holds the prize*
> *So wait and doubt no longer.*

"Commence to possess" to-day! Why wait longer? See here is power; what doth hinder thee possessing it? And here too is spiritual wealth, why linger longer in the domain of bankruptcy? Thou art empty and needy! Then at once plunge into the limitless, shoreless ocean of His provision. Stand no more starving when the fat of the land is at your command. Is there a garment that you will not find in the royal wardrobe? Is there a weapon that the heavenly armoury does not contain? What are thy needs? Name them, and though they be legion in number, yet I warrant thee that this storehouse will yield all that thou canst desire of spiritual blessing. "Every place that the sole of your foot shall tread upon *shall be yours*." Do you believe it? If so, then the land lies before thee, and the days of thy mourning are for ever ended.

Rev. E. W. Moore, in his admirable little book, *The Christ-Controlled Life*, tells of an estate in Yorkshire, the owner of which died in the workhouse, whereas his successor was rolling in wealth. He asks the pertinent question, "Why was it?" The new owner had discovered a copper-mine in the grounds, which had brought him his prosperity. The copper-mine was there all the time, yet the former owner – who had just as much title to its wealth as the present one – had died in poverty, unable to meet his liabilities. It is often so with the Lord's people – the spiritual treasure is there, but it remains undiscovered, unappropriated. "How can He but, in giving Him, lavish on us all things?" (Rom. viii. 32, Weymouth).

Hearken to the all-sufficient assurance, *"I have given . . . !"* Let it nerve thee to noble endeavour.

> *Arouse thy courage ere it fails and faints*
> *God props no Gospel up with sinking saints.*

Possess our Possessions

It is recorded of Joshua that he "took the whole land." Shall we not be equally bold in our faith and not linger listlessly and impotently upon the frontiers of all this fulness?

The Marquess of Salisbury was criticised for his Colonial politics and replied: "Gentlemen, get larger maps." The people of God need similar expansion in their outlook and uplook.

"But suppose!" Ah, supposition has been responsible for much failure in Christian life; it has led many a soul back from the very verge of victory, back to darkness, despair and defeat. "But perhaps!" Yes, these are twin temptations which often hang on the heels of those who contemplate the conquest of Canaan. My dear friend, if you are willing to be robbed of your spiritual birthright by any such specious suggestions as these – well then, your folly is great. Suppose, indeed! Suppose what? Can God fail? Is His Word true? When He speaks, does He mean what He says?

> *Faint-heart the Devil loves to make*
> *Tremble with "Only suppose";*
> *Strong purpose says, "I onward press,*
> *I trust Him and He knows."*

Think of the unclaimed and unconquered secrets of the prayer life. Here is ample scope for those who wish to excel in exploit for God. The possibilities of prayer are without number – stake your claim to larger possessions in this wonderful realm of achievement. Think of the perishing pagan in [many lands]. Shall we not possess them for Him? Let us claim the heathen for His inheritance, and the uttermost parts of the earth for His possession. Consider the stubborn strongholds of evil that need levelling to the ground before the Gospel – bring this wonderful prayer pressure to bear upon them, and they will collapse, and be possessed for God.

"Rise up!" That is to say, be on the move, take action, launch out, bestir thyself. Commandeer all thy faculties for a holy and aggressive alliance to capture the spiritual spoil which awaits the dauntless and daring soul. Those words should spur to the highest and utmost in the Christian life – should serve as a stimulus to live valorously and victoriously for Christ.

Dr J. R. Miller has observed that "we fail many times to receive the blessing He has ready for us, because we do not go forward with Him. While we miss much good through not waiting for God, we also miss much through *over-waiting*. There are times when our strength is to sit still, but there are also times when we are to go forward with a firm step."

Love's Miracles

Thou art the Way to "more abundant" life;
Each step leads on to life more blest.

Again what a world of wealth the Word of God offers to the diligent student who digs deep into its depths. Perhaps that sacred Book is largely sealed to you. "Rise up" and enter into the enjoyment of its blood-bought heritage. Commence to possess its priceless promises – feed upon its life-giving truths. Think of some of the doors which the hand of the Lord has thrown open to us. Doors into a life of victory and intimate union with Himself. Doors into more powerful and fruitful ministry.

All things are possible! Glorious word!
Eye hath not seen them, and ear hath not heard;
Neither hath entered the heart to conceive
Things that are possible – if we believe!

When I am dying, how glad I shall be
That the lamp of my life has been blazed out for Thee;
I shall not mind then whatever I gave
Of labour, or money, one sinner to save.
I shall not mind that the way has been rough,
That Thy dear feet led me – that will be enough.
When I am dying how glad I shall be
That the lamp of my life has been blazed out for Thee.

PASSION

*Your spirits should be fairly seething with enthusiasm while you
are toiling as the Lord's bondsmen. – Romans xii. 11 (A. S. Way).*

> *Lord, make me a flame,*
> *As I minister to Thee;*
> *A burning fiery flame*
> *I want to be;*
> *A flame to spread the fire*
> *Of Holy Ghost desire.*

FOR life to achieve its greatest glory and reach its highest
spiritual consummation it must first of all be invested with
the sovereign passion of love for the Master. This must become
the dominant and directing force, the all-sufficient energy, the driving impulse, the propelling power, the sceptre that holds the throne
of the heart and brings the whole being under its blessed sway. This
princely passion will make the stammering tongue eloquent, giving
courage to the timid heart, and steadiness to the faltering feet. And
then issuing from this passion for Christ must come a passion for
souls – a passion to serve and save. Zinzendorf's great love for Christ
is expressed in those historic words, "I have but one passion – it is
He." And this saintly man became the founder of the Moravian Mission.

The Holy Spirit as a driving energy is symbolised by wind and
water. In this connection think of Niagara's mighty falls, and the terrific and terrible force those waters represent. That vast power has
been harnessed by man to such an extent that today it drives the machinery and supplies the light of many a distant city. How much greater
is the dynamic of the Holy Ghost. When man is in contact with this
heavenly dynamo, a spiritual voltage is generated which, in the execution of the Divine will, makes him proof against all opposition.

And then how blessedly contagious is this heaven-born passion. How it thaws the frostbound atmosphere, melting indifference, indolence and indulgence. Like a gushing fountain of sparkling water it rises up and cleanses every fellowship which it adorns. How quickly it transforms the impassive, irresponsive community into a glad and genial assembly.

The Word of God declares, "Without faith it is impossible to please Him." Would it not be equally true to add that without this God-breathed passion it is both impossible to please Him perfectly or satisfy Him fully? If we are to form an estimate of the Divine mind from the words of the risen Lord in Revelation iii. 16, then certainly we shall conclude that He loathes lukewarmness; that the tepid type of Christianity, of which alas, there is all too much, is something most offensive to the mind of God. It is the boiling, blazing, bubbling believer that honours God and whom God honours. Half-heartedness brings discredit upon the name of Christ and disqualifies those In whom it is manifest. Christianity is more than a profession, it is a passion – a possession.

Shew me the man, in any realm, who has forged to the front, who has made his ministry a memorial for generations to come – the man who has defied difficulties, overcome whole legions of obstacles, and even attempted and achieved what others counted impossible – and you will discover in that man one who was possessed of an invincible and irresistible passion. He may have had severe handicaps: failings that placed him at a considerable disadvantage, and gave his fellow competitors in life's race distinct and decided advantage, but the one redeeming and qualifying feature was his burning passion. He may have made mistakes, and his too precipitate action nearly involved him in disaster, yet his unquenchable and unconquerable passion saved him from defeat: it carried him through when others staggered and succumbed. Perhaps driven a score of times from his heart's objective, and yet on-borne by the overmastering passion, he returns to the conquest of his goal.

Who were the men that lit world fires? Who have moved and melted thousands? Whose voice stirred the sleeping conscience of nations? – men in whom all those magnificent and heroic Christian virtues found their highest and utmost form of expression? Who are these that have scaled achievement's most dizzy heights, and descended to the deepest depth of sacrifice, drinking the bitter cup of reproach and rejection to the very dregs? Are they not those who were mastered by this love-passion for Christ? Souls who feared not to face death in the cause of their Master? Men who blazed the path for the Gospel, and planted the blood-red banner of the Cross in the very heart of the enemy's territory? Were they not passion-possessed men? Men whose being burnt for God with undying flame? Thomas Cook says that "passion stirs passion, emotion kindles emotion, and only men who are at white heat make any deep and lasting impression."

> *Oh for a passionate love for souls,*
> *Oh for a love that burns,*
> *Oh for a love that loves unto death,*
> *Oh for a soul that yearns!*

John Welsh, that saintly soul-lover and soul-winner, would sometimes awaken his wife in the night by his weeping, and when she asked him why he wept he would answer, "I have the souls of three thousand persons to answer for, and I don't know how it is with many of them." It is recorded of Alexander Duff, who, as Dr A. T. Pierson tells us, "ranks with Carey and Livingstone as one of the great missionary triad of the nineteenth century," that he "made the very pulse of missions to beat quicker, shaping missionary effort and moving hundreds to go, as well as tens of thousands to give. His short career was like a prairie fire, sweeping hot and fast over the land. The enthusiasm he kindled was intense and glowing."

Of Raymond Lull, pioneer to the Mahometans, it is recorded that "he dared a Red Sea of blood for the sake of following the 'vision.'" Ignatius, one of the noble army of martyrs, cried, "Come, fire and iron, and grapplings with wild beasts, cuttings and manglings, wrenchings of bones, hacking of limbs, crushing of my whole body; come, cruel torture of the Devil, to assail me – only be it mine to attain unto Jesus Christ." Francis Xavier, that red-hot missionary, cried out in his magnificent zeal, "Whatever be the form of torture or of death that awaits me, I am ready to suffer it ten thousand times for my Lord's sake." Then think of Wesley and Whitefield, of Bunyan and Brainerd, of Moffatt and Martyn, and a host of others.

Do you wonder that such passion, such devotion, such surrender, led to triumphs that have helped to make Christian history of which the perusal thrills us in the twentieth century?

Nothing can compensate for the absence of this vital passion. It is written of one well-known political figure that he possessed "every quality for the first rank, and for the foremost place in that rank, save the one urgent passion of enthusiasm." This disqualified him for leadership. C.H. Spurgeon says in his lectures to his students: "In many instances ministerial success is traceable almost entirely to an intense zeal, a consuming passion for souls, and an eager enthusiasm in the cause of God." How powerless is passionless preaching – 'tis true it may be theologically correct, and doctrinally sound, and couched in the finest language, yet it resembles the cold beauty of the lifeless marble. It invites indifference and induces somnolence. It fails to move the people to whom it is preached because it has failed to stir our own souls. O servant of God, ask Him to make you desperate in your endeavour to win those who are drifting to their doom!

> *Descend from heaven, celestial Dove,*
> *With flames of pure seraphic love;*
> *Warm our cold hearts with heavenly heat,*
> *And set our souls on fire.*

When we speak of passion we have in mind that divinely imparted quality which is permanent in the life. Not the result of some stirring of life's surface, but the steady glow of an inward fire, lit by the hand of God and fed from the same source – a Divine heat that radiates from within, and therefore strong enough to resist all the freezing, hardening influences without. To be enduring it must be born of a great and growing conviction, and constantly fed by an ever-deepening apprehension of the faithfulness of God – something that grips life at its very centre; not that which is merely fitful, that bursts into brilliant flame for a season, giving an occasional upheaval of fervour, and then anon disappoints by its sudden disappearance. Passion is the antithesis of sentimentality, and it burns up all that which nauseates. There is a healthy tone about it. Speaking of enthusiasm, Sterling tells us that it is "grave, inward, self-controlled; while mere excitement is outward, fantastical, hysterical."

Then, also, our giving should be instinct with passion. The giving of our time, our talents, our children, our money – ourselves. Think of God's great passion for the bestowal of Himself on the world which He loved. View it in the wonder light of Golgotha; see it revealed in its crimson glory on Calvary's crest; look upon those blood-drops of anguish as they stream from the Saviour's thorn-crowned brow. And thus learn somewhat of the intensity of love's power to give without reserve or restraint. When the true love-fires burn within we shall develop a hunger for giving. Then the treasury of the temple will be full to overflow, and the work of the Lord will not suffer for lack of funds. We recently read of a poor Russian widow woman who gave a rouble to the Bible Society, and when asked whether such a sum was not rather too much for one in her circumstances, she answered, "Love is not afraid of giving too much."

Oh for a mighty wave of holy, heavenly passion! The pastor,

the evangelist, the missionary, the Sunday School teacher, the open-air worker – they all need it. Perhaps you say, "My heart is cold and unmoved; no fire burns upon the altar within; I have no great mental power, no genius. Had I but the pen of a poet, or the tongue of an orator – but I possess neither." You ask, "What can I do to procure and promote this passion in my life?" Seek a personal Baptism of the Holy Ghost, that will supply and sustain this "seething enthusiasm." And then go down to life's sea of suffering and sorrow, and look upon its heaving bosom, and contemplate those who are struggling in its depths. Look until the fountains of the deep within are broken up; until your message and ministry become charged with a passion to save; until your whole soul catches fire. Let the vision of a lost world grip you. Go and look upon the fields already white unto harvest; behold the precious sheaves that are even now perishing for lack of labourers. Look until the holy compulsion seizes you, and you are constrained to plunge in to the rescue. Vision will bring passion; the Divine urge will be born out of the unveiled need. Mrs Albert Head prayed, "Stir me, oh! stir me, Lord, I care not how; but stir my heart in passion for the world." And Mr Aitkin's prayer was, "Lord, take my lips and speak through them; take my mind and think through it – take my heart and set it on fire." Make this the cry of your heart, and God will answer with fire from on high.

> *Devoted, desirous,*
> *Lord, we yearn;*
> *Fire us, inspire us,*
> *Till we burn.*

Paul's passion is seen in his magnificent challenge in Romans viii. 35: "Who shall separate us from the love of Christ? Shall tribulation, or distress, or persecution, or famine, or nakedness, or peril, or sword?" No power could fright this dauntless soul in whom burned this holy love-fire. He writes to Timothy, and the word he uses is of a fierce struggle – Young translates it "agony" – passion, the old word used for our Lord's agony. In the next chapter he urges still further, "Stir into flame the gift within thee." It is said of Praying Hyde, the man whose intercession "changed things" for the Sialkot Revival, that "it was evident to all that he was bowed down with sore travail of soul. He missed many meals, and when I went to his room I would find him lying as in great agony, or walking up and down as if an inward fire were burning in his bones." And so there was that fire of which our Lord spoke when He said, "I came to cast fire upon the earth, and what will I if it be already kindled! But I have a baptism to be baptised with, and how am I straitened till it be accomplished!"

We are living in an age when there is an abundance of the artificial; almost anything can be imitated in these days. And we are in danger of being satisfied with a merely imaginary enthusiasm. But of what use is an imitation fire? You will get no real warmth from it. It will not arrest the progress of unbelief. It takes real Holy Ghost fire to change the frozen conditions that often obtain in so many circles. We must have meetings that are permeated with power – testimonies that are throbbing with life – lives that are lit with the glory of God. Anything but this deadening, damning nonchalance. The period in which we live demands a personal, positive, passionate, and aggressive evangelism – an enthusiasm that will sweep its way through every opposing force.

> *Burn on, O fire within my heart,*
> *Burn fiercely night and day,*
> *Till all the dross of earthly love*
> *Is burned and burned away.*

God guides by His Word. He also guides by circumstances, and by the Spirit; there is no royal road to guidance; God's clarifier in guidance is waiting; sometimes it is extraordinary; sometimes ordinary; guides a step at a time; it is maybe by stops as well as by steps; it is cumulative ; beware of short cuts in guidance and of flesh and blood guidance; guidance is sure for those who wait and pray.

DIVINELY DIRECTED

Take step by step by the Spirit. – Galatians v. 25 (Moule).

Side by side we know not whither
But with whom we know full well;
Side by side henceforth for ever,
With Thee, veiled Emmanuel.

IT is well sometimes to take a steady gaze at the past years – years that have held much of mingled sunshine and shadow, silence and song, pain and pleasure, loss and gain. As we look back in many respects we find that the past has not proved all that we had hoped. There has been more of the battle than the banquet, more of the clamour than the calm, more trial than triumph. Mixed with many of life's festivities has been the bitterness of deep disappointment. Too many jarring discords have marred the music of our ministry.

Thought stirs within us a great yearning after better things in the future. We long to gain from experience the secrets of success. Possibly the friction and failure of the past has been largely due to the uncontrolled "steps" that we have taken. Let me but take one self-prompted step, and I shall discover ere long that a barrier has arisen which if allowed to remain, will impoverish the whole of my life. It has been in our moments of unwariness that our feet have found some false track, and thus have been diverted from the heavenly course. It is in such seasons that we have embarked upon those hazardous enterprises which have ended in catastrophe. How careful we should be to look to the Lord when entering into any relationship that affects our future. How watchful in all things to acknowledge His right to lead. "Step by step" suggests close companionship with Christ – a walk with God which reduces the possibility of wandering to a minimum. A life so regulated by Divine wisdom – a heart that readily responds to the Divine touch, even as the needle turns to the pole, needing not the painful pressure of hard circumstances to bend it to obedience, but always inclines to the Divine will. This exquisite spiritual sensitiveness Godward is the spring of a life that is large and lovely. If we are to accept the Lordship of Christ then this means that He must hold the reins, determining the route and regulating the pace. And, as one writer has reminded us, "You can command God because you utterly obey Him . . . you can say, 'I can, because God can.'" Life becomes profoundly powerful because it is thus brought into and kept in union with the Inexhaustible and Irresistible. And life becomes profoundly blessed under these conditions. The soul can then sing:

> *And now I have flung myself fearlessly out,*
> *Like a chip on the stream of the Infinite Will;*
> *I pass the rough rocks with a smile and a shout,*
> *And I just let my Lord His dear purpose fulfil.*

Perhaps on the surface of things, and looking on life as a whole, one would be tempted to regard "one step" as of very little consequence. And yet serious thought reveals that all life's subsequent steps are vitally affected by the movement of the moment. "Before entering into any alliance – taking a partner in life, going into a business with another, yielding assent to any proposition which involves confederation with others – be sure to ask counsel at the mouth of the Lord. He will assuredly answer by an irresistible impulse; by a circumstance strange and unexpected; by a passage of Scripture. He will choose His own messenger; but He will send a message." When the history of life is reviewed from the vantage point of eternity, we shall then see the value of the "single" steps that we have taken.

> *Only a step may sever, pole-wide, future and past.*
> *Only a touch may rivet links which for life shall last.*

In America lies what is known as the Great Divide. A drop of water falling on one side of this makes its way to the Pacific Ocean. If it falls on the other it flows eastward till it reaches the Atlantic. How this speaks to us of the need of obeying the inspired injunction which heads this chapter. We are all anxious to reach the goal and to win the prize of a victorious life in Christ. Then let us see to it that all our steps are carefully guarded. That each new step is taken in entire dependence upon the Lord. How rich and radiant in spiritual treasure will the hours and days of our life be if all our steps are directed by the Lord. God wants to build the temple of our life not in a moment, but moment by moment. Great things are of slow and steady growth. "A toadstool springs up in a night – an oak grows in a hundred years. But then it is an oak." "His way" must lead to perfected life-ministries – perfect in the senses of completion and consecration.

Often our point of focus is wrong. We are in danger of putting too great an emphasis upon the high and heroic things of life, overlooking those of lesser magnitude. And yet ofttimes Christian heroism finds a finer field of service and sacrifice amid the smaller circle of opportunity. When some really important step is contemplated we give ourselves to prayer lest we should make a false move. But is it not equally essential to take each step with our eyes upon Jesus, thus forming the habit of reliance upon Him in all things? Make it a practice to talk to God about everything, however apparently trivial, that in any way affects our lives. This will eliminate that erratic expression of God, and enable us to move with steady precision to the Divine destination. We shall then,

> *Step by step divinely guided*
> *Through the untried future way;*
> *Step by step as children learning*
> *Hold their father's hand to pray.*

> *Day by day in prompt obedience,*
> *Swift to hear and quick to learn;*
> *Homeward, heavenward, God-directed,*
> *Looking for His quick return,*

no longer be driven by impulse to action which often costs us heavily in humiliating consequences. What issues often hang upon our speedy response to the voice or the touch of the Holy Ghost. As we thus move onward with God, life will be "girt about with miracle." Many a desert bush will burst forth into beneficent flame, making a land of loneliness a place of wondrous vision, from which the voice of God speaks in pentecostal power. Henceforth we shall enjoy a God-guided, God-guarded, God-governed experience. Our course will always be upward – homeward, heavenward, throneward.

> *Thou wilt shew me, mighty Father,*
> *Step by step the wondrous way;*
> *Side by side, thro' Time's long twilight,*
> *Press we to the dawning day.*

The Word of God contains so many precious promises of guidance. Think of that one in Psalm xxxii. 8: "I will guide thee with Mine eye." Of course this demands constant attention – always looking off unto Him for that directing vision which shall keep our feet from the perilous place. Like the Psalmist, our eyes must be "ever toward the Lord." There must be no wandering vision, lest we stumble and miss the pathway of His purpose. Do not forget that "where God's finger points, God's hand will make the way."

Dr. Meyer recalls an experience which occurred when crossing the Irish Channel on a dark, starless night. He says, "I stood on the deck by the captain and asked him, 'How do you know the Holyhead Harbour on so dark a night as this?' He said, 'You see those three lights? Those three must line up behind each other as one, and when we see them so united we know the exact position of the harbour's mouth.'" He continued, "when we want to know God's will there are three things which always occur – the inward impulse, the Word of God, and the trend of circumstances. God in the heart impelling you forward; God in His Book corroborating whatever He says in the heart; and God in circumstances, which are always indicative of His will. Never start until these three things agree." Thus God hedges in the sincere soul so that he may not miss the way of His will.

"Mine eyes are perpetually directed unto Jehovah," says the inspired writer. Blessed indeed is the life that is thus enthralled – caught in the glorious attraction from on high. As the flower turns its face to the sun, drawn by the irresistible lure of those life-giving rays, so the soul instinctively responds to the Divine captivation, and in so doing becomes a glad partaker of the wealth and warmth which stream from the Eternal Throne. The believer who thus possesses the trained vision – the focal point of whose entire life is always and only in God – can never know the bitterness of spiritual blindness or bondage. To him life is large and magnificent in meaning and eternal in its scope. Such souls cannot be overpowered by the winds of temptation or swallowed up in the seas of difficulty; to them all things are equally possible to God; the glory of His face is the abundant compensation for every cross that is carried – the sufficient incentive and inspiration to every enterprise and exploit that is attempted – the essential and vital equipment for every ministry to which the Divine Will calls. This vision glorious is the welcome assurance of the fulfilment of every heaven-given promise – the essence of that face to face unveiling which will be ours in the day of His power. To look in any other direction is to invite fear and failure.

Divinely Directed

The Lord will go before thee! and the cloud thou
deemest thine
May disperse before it reach thee, by the touch of
the Love Divine.

What comfort and courage that promise inspires, "As thou goest 'step by step' the way shall open up before thee." God's directing hand shall lead us on "stepping in the light," until at last we emerge into heaven's glorious throne-lit realm. As thus we move with God we shall find our circle of service ever enlarging. Beginning at Jerusalem, we shall by-and-by find our ministry leads us to Judea, and from thence to Samaria. How many whose names stand high in the esteem of their fellows for their work's sake, have commenced their ministry in the Sunday School, serving their ministerial apprenticeship with a handful of tiny tots whom they sought to win for Jesus. There was laid the foundation of many a life-work which has splendidly contributed to the annals of Christian heroism. Mr. Hudson Taylor served his apprenticeship for his great and glorious future amid the slums of Hull, seeking to save the perishing souls of that city in which he laboured for a living. There it was he learnt those early lessons of faith which in subsequent years enabled him to believe God so magnificently for the supply of the needs of that important work which he had undertaken for the Lord and Christless China. "Step by step" the Spirit of God led him on from one venture of trust to another yet greater than the last. Deeper and deeper grew his confidence in Jehovah, and more marked became the proofs of Divine power.

Dr. Jowett in one of his books has called attention to the fact that "a guide-post is one thing, a guide is another." And, he adds, "It is helpful to have written instructions; it is far more helpful to have the leadership of a companionable friend." What a joy to know that God has not merely issued directions for the journey, but He has provided every traveller to Zion with a wonderful Leader and Director in the Person of the Holy Spirit. And we must not forget that it is only as we walk with the Lord that we can be "workers together with Him."

What comfort comes into the perplexed and pained heart when the Spirit speaks such assuring words as those found in Isaiah lviii. 11: "The Lord shall guide thee *continually* and satisfy thy soul in drought." Not sometimes, on special occasions, but continually – all the way, and all the time. And when we come to the conclusion of life's journey we shall see how the Lord has led us in right paths.

Love's Miracles

And the pathway on earth God barred, we shall know
was no mistake,
Aye, this we shall know, and more, when the dawn of
that Day shall break!

The great feature which distinguished the life of Enoch, making it stand out with striking boldness against the background of mediocrity of his period, was that "He walked with God," or as the Hebrew might be correctly translated, "He *caused* himself to walk with God." In other words, it became his life ambition – the sovereign aspiration of his soul – to company with the Eternal God. By an act of his will he put himself into alignment with the Divine purpose and plan, and by a sustained attitude of spirit that union was maintained through those long years of pilgrimage, until eventually he was translated. Each new step taken in the pathway planned by the heart of God meant a deepening consciousness of His wonderful wisdom, bringing fresh proofs of the unfailing goodness of the Lord. Enoch *dared* to walk with God, even though by so doing he ran the risk of coming into conflict with popular life and thought.

What a priceless privilege to walk with God! To move in harmony with the glorified Emmanuel! All fear removed in the assurance of His guidance. How beautiful is Spurrell's translation of Job xxiii. 11 – "In His steps will I firmly fix my feet."

Let this be the unchanging determination of our lives "until He come."

And now "my Home is God," and sheltered there,
God meets the trials of my earthly life;
God compasses me round from storm and strife;
God takes the burden of my daily care.
O wondrous Place! O Home divinely fair!
And I, God's little one, safe hidden there.
Lord, as I dwell in Thee and Thou in me,
So make me dead to everything but Thee;
That as I rest within my Home most fair,
My soul may evermore and only see
My God in everything and everywhere;
My Home is God.

A CURE FOR CARE

Look not around. – Isaiah xli. 10.
He considered not. – Romans iv. 19.

What though there're mountains before you
That progress seem to delay ?
If the other side God should need you,
With Him there's always a way;
The mountains of hindrance arising,
At His word become a plain,
And there's always a purpose behind
For the time that they do remain.

LOOK not around! To remain unmoved by one's visible environment! To stand perfectly still in the midst of annoying, agitating influences! Doubtless this is one of the most difficult lessons to learn as well as one of the most desirable traits to cultivate in the Christian character. When passing through some severe and strange phase of Divine discipline, how strong the temptation to look around" – to survey our surroundings and seek to gather from them the inspiration and incentive which can alone come from the Lord Himself. Naturally we are disposed to depend upon the sensible rather than the spiritual, the temporal more than the eternal, devoting too much attention to that which often is not fundamentally essential to the accomplishment of God's purpose. How sadly inadequate and inaccurate is the human estimate of things; potent factors in the outworking of the Divine will are frequently minimised or altogether lost sight of, whilst things which are almost irrelevant to the thought of God are magnified to the greatest extent; emphasis is laid upon natural resources whilst the supernatural are overlooked. Says the cold, calculating, deductive mind, "What are they among so many?" A comparison of the great and pressing need with the meagre supplies available leads to a conclusion of unbelief. In an extremity how quickly we commence to tabulate the things upon which we can count for assistance; a certain amount of satisfaction may thus be gleaned, but generally we discover that what we can do and how far we can go is quite unequal to the occasion, with the result that ere long we are led to exclaim in the fearfulness of our hearts, "Who is sufficient for this thing?" Happy, indeed, is that soul which, having learnt to "consider not" those things that are, counting them as though they were not, is now able triumphantly to assert, "Our sufficiency is of God."

This leads us to observe that in the pathway of Christian discipleship –

Circumstances must not be unduly considered. God gives a promise which reason adjudges only possible of fulfilment under certain propitious circumstances. We have to learn that God's authority and ability to perform His promises is not subject to circumstances of any kind, that He is able to do the "exceeding abundant" thing anywhere and at any time. The continual remembrance and recognition of this fact should serve to steady the staggering soul, and enable it to regain its spiritual equipoise even amid the most challenging circumstances. The handful of meal and the cruse of oil in the house of the widow of Zarephath represented circumstances sufficient to overthrow the strongest faith. And yet these were the means employed by Jehovah to work His will. It was not by these altogether insufficient supplies that the prophet was to measure the Divine power or estimate the Divine faithfulness – to contemplate these things was to expose himself to the danger of losing heart – but behind and beyond these Elijah saw *God.* Gideon's little army when measured by the might of Midian must have appeared contemptible indeed. Before such overwhelming odds such a mere handful of men could not hope to stand. And yet God gave victory to His people. How often the Divine hand upsets all carnal calculations, working His miracles through minorities, that no flesh should glory in His presence.

> *For faith grows but by exercise*
> *In circumstance impossible.*

Napoleon once said, "God is on the side of the heaviest artillery." But at Waterloo he found that he was mistaken, for the 160 guns of the British overcame the 250 guns of the French. Again, "when Napoleon was contemplating his great march on Moscow, he explained his plans to a lady in a very haughty and boastful manner. 'Please be reverent,' said the lady; 'for man proposes, but God disposes.' 'Madam,' said the proud Corsican, 'I will propose and dispose too.' But he forgot God was over all. A few months later the lesson was driven home to him as he beat a disastrous retreat from Moscow. We cannot defeat God's purposes. His sovereign will shall be done."

> Say not, my soul, "From whence can God relieve my care?"
> Remember that Omnipotence has servants everywhere.
> His wisdom is sublime, His heart supremely kind;
> God never is before His time, and never is behind.

Circumstances may be and often are most misleading, and therefore cannot be relied upon to guide us in moments of perplexity; they may play a contributory part in indicating the mind of the Lord, but should never be taken solely as the basis of faith. In our endeavour to arrive at the Divine thought on any point the Word of God must always take precedence. Let us not forget that the enemy has power to create critical circumstances which appear absolutely contradictory to the assurance which God has implanted within the soul; these if regarded will lead out of the pathway of power and blessing, into what may prove nothing more than a cul-de-sac. Do not overlook the fact that although faith may not change our circumstances, yet it will give us the mastery of them.

Again, circumstances may suddenly develop sufficiently to cause grave concern, circumstances which threaten to imperil the very enterprise to which the Holy Ghost constrained. Christ commissions His newly formed Church to the task of establishing and extending His Kingdom. Almost ere they had commenced their work, a perfect hurricane of persecution broke upon them, and the whole company of Christians were scattered. It seemed as though all their work was destined to be swallowed up in the flood of bitterness let loose upon them. And yet this was God's way of expansion and increase. The wind of persecution scattered the seed of Divine truth, carrying it into other fields where it soon took root.

To remain consistent to the Divine call we cannot afford to "look around" – let us see in this sudden change of conditions another subtle attempt of Satan to divert us from the course, and thus cause us to miss the mark and forfeit the prize of a victorious life in the Lord. How many Christian lives, at one time so full of promise, have been shipwrecked upon the jagged rocks of cruel circumstances.

> All your anxiety, all your care
> Bring to the mercy seat, leave it there.

Love's Miracles

Never a burden He cannot bear,
Never a Friend like Jesus.

Again consequences should not be considered. To obey the
commands of Christ means sacrifice; a pathway of blood opens up
before the would-be follower of Jesus; thorns and tears are his guerdon
here; his life will be stamped with the offensive stigma of the Cross;
he will bear in his ministry the marks which distinguish him as a
servant of the "Man of Calvary." But surely love is equal to loss and
prepared for suffering. To turn away from the proffered cup because
it contains the bitterness of rejection only betrays an absence of that
vital devotion which enables the ardent soul to "endure all things" in
its allegiance to Christ. The suffering consequent upon acceptance of
the Cross is far outweighed by the "more excellent glory" which
streams into the soul of the abandoned saint. To allow the consequences of complete consecration to deter you from "pressing on the
upward way" is indicative of the existence of a strong self-life which
is ready to compromise in order to avoid the odium of those who
walk not in the counsel of the Lord. If you yield yourself to God as a
whole burnt-offering, certainly you must be prepared for consequences
which will teach you the meaning and value of crucifixion. Perchance
the circle of your friends may grow considerably smaller. It may mean
financial loss in that lucrative business in which you have hitherto
been so prosperous. But what if it does? Are not the compensations
far greater than the losses? Beloved, "consider not" these things!
Rather regard the abundant honour of a closer walk with God! Why,
the Lord Himself shall be your "exceeding great Reward!" And
"greater things than these" will He do for you!

When the woes of life o' ertake me,
Hopes deceive and fears annoy,
Never shall the Cross forsake me
Lo! it glows with peace and joy.

Moreover, *there are times when capacity should not be considered.* Do we not learn that God hath chosen the "things which are
not, to bring to nought the things that are"? Has not Jehovah often
called men to service for which to all human appearances they had no
aptitude? And has He not wonderfully glorified Himself in the manner in which they have achieved success? To consider our compe-
tence would often prevent us from obeying the call of God! Are not
the thought of our heart and the language of our lips expressed in the
words of Jeremiah, "Ah, Lord God! behold I cannot speak: for I am a

child"? And yet who knows but what *our very weakness has safe-guarded us from defeat*; in our weakness the Lord has shewn Himself strong. God is able of the most unlikely material to make the choicest vessels, and through the most unskilled channels to produce the rarest results. Therefore do not permit the paucity of your natural endowments to prevent you from doing great things for God. Natural gifts do not always qualify for the highest attainments in the Kingdom of God.

"It is told of Leonardo da Vinci that while still a pupil, before his genius burst into brilliance . . . he received a special inspiration in this way: his old and famous master, because of the growing infirmities of age, felt obliged to give up his work, and one day bade da Vinci finish for him a picture which he had begun. The young man had such a reverence for his master's skill that he shrank from the task. The old artist, however, would not accept any excuse, but persisted in his command, saying, 'Do your best!' Da Vinci at last tremblingly seized the brush, and kneeling before the easel, prayed, "It is for the sake of my beloved master that I implore skill and power for this undertaking." As he proceeded with his task his hand grew steady, his eye awoke with slumbering genius. He forgot himself, and was filled with enthusiasm for his work. When the painting was finished, the old master was carried into the studio to pass judgment on the result. His eyes rested on a triumph of art. Throwing his arms about the young artist, he exclaimed, 'My son, I paint no more.'"

"Consider not" thy lack of ability! "Look not around" upon what thou art or what thou hast! Remember the greatness of thy God and take heart! Your nothingness linked on to God's Almightiness is more than a match for all the forces of darkness which are allied against thee! Refuse no call that God gives because you feel unequal to it! Seek neither in yourself nor in your circumstances to find a reason for the Divine choice. Jehovah makes no mistakes! Give yourself up to God and He will work in you both to will and to do of His good pleasure.

Live Thou in me! –
All hindrances remove, that I be made
A channel just through which Thy life conveyed
May be, and Thou alone be manifest–
That others seeing Thee be helped and blessed;
Live Thou in me; O Lord, Thy child inspire
With Thine own Spirit as with sacred fire!

How wonderfully carefree God can keep the trustful soul, bringing it to a place of tranquillity in Himself. Anxious for nothing because prayerful and praiseful for everything. The eye ever looking upward for the supply of every need, conscious that out of the Divine abundance a constant stream of blessing will flow. Built around such a life is that invisible yet impenetrable pavilion of the Divine presence – God's all-powerful protection from the incoming flood of evil.

We are thinking now of one who in the midst of the perplexities and perils of a hostile heathen land wrote, "these dangers, difficulties and trials, while leading to a deeper realisation of our own weakness, poverty and need, will constrain us also to lean more constantly, to draw more largely, to rest more implicitly on the strength, the riches, the fulness of Jesus." Thus God teaches His children the lesson of utter freedom from anxious care. "Troubled on every side, yet not distressed; perplexed, but not in despair; persecuted, but not forsaken; cast down, but not destroyed." Possessing an answer to every challenge of the enemy, we move on in the train of His triumph from "victory unto victory."

But you are a chosen race, a priesthood of kingly lineage, a holy nation, a people belonging specially to God. — I Peter ii. 9 (Weymouth).
And they shall be unto Me a special treasure. — Malachi iii. 17 (Spurrell).

HIS

My Beloved is mine, and I am His.
Song of Solomon ii. 16.

I am the Lord's: O joy beyond expression,
O sweet response to voice of love Divine;
Faith's joyous "Yes" to the assuring whisper,
"Fear not; I have redeemed thee; thou art Mine."

IN surveying the wonderful position of power and privilege which we as children of God occupy, it is intended that we should endeavour to realise afresh how absolutely and completely we actually belong to the Lord. Happy indeed will the writer be should he succeed, in making more clear to some disconsolate heart how strong are the ties which bind us to Christ – how deeply and eternally we are His.

In the first place shall we observe *that we are His by the power of a Divine choice.* "He chose us . . . for His own" (Eph. i. 4, A. S. Way). "The Lord . . . hath chosen thee . . . unto Himself" (Deut. vii. 6).

If it has not already done so, may the music of this glad assurance steal softly and sweetly into our hearts, pervading our lives with its rich spiritual resonance. The writer well remembers the hour when the revelation of this great fact dawned upon him; it is now many years ago, but the memory of that blessed occasion still sheds its fragrance over his life.

This choice of His finds its response, and we are His by the longing of our own heart and will. We chose Him because He first chose us – we are His by the seal and sanction of our own great responding love. He has completely conquered and claimed us as His own; freely does our heart acknowledge His ownership – "Whose I am and Whom I serve." Out of the apprehension of this glorious fact springs a life of sanctified service.

God grant that any who have not yet entered into the enjoyment of knowing that they are "His" may do so immediately. Live no longer in uncertainty – claim this assurance Divine – it is your heritage.

In Macaulay's *History of England* we are told that during the Commonwealth days, Cromwell wanted to be made King of England. But the aristocracy and the soldiers would not have him to reign over them. They knew, however, that unless Cromwell was at the head of affairs, everything would soon go all wrong again in England. So they said they would not make him King to reign over them, but if he liked they would make him Lord High Protector to guide and counsel and defend them. One writer in applying this fact of history, says, "Is not that a picture of the way in which many people treat Jesus? They are so afraid of the consequences of their own sins, and so anxious about the future, that they want Him as Lord High Protector to save them, but they will not have Him King to reign over them." How true is all this. And yet to those who have caught a glimpse of His beauty, the heart wholly responds, and lovingly accepts His Lordship and Kingship over the life.

Furthermore we rejoice to realise that we are His by reason of a Divine union. "He that is joined to the Lord is one spirit" (I Cor. vi. 17). Whether we consider this union under the inspired figure of a body, with all the members fitly framed together, or as a vine, each branch of which shares in the common life, or again as a bride whose life is so inseparably interwoven with that of her bridegroom, we see how vitally and essentially we are united to our Lord. Although the union may be invisible, yet it is nevertheless indissoluble. It is possible that this union may be so real to us that not a desire divides – not a shadow separates – not a cloud veils the face of God. A union which perhaps finds its fullest expression in our likeness to Him to whom our hearts are wedded. It is said that "on one occasion when Jenny Lind, the celebrated singer, was recovering from a long and severe illness she wrote to an author thanking him for one of his books. 'The passage,' she said, 'across to the other side appeared to me so easy and so beautiful; the true home, after which I was longing, seemed so heavenly, that everything earthly in me – all anguish, all grief, all the countless sufferings of a very sensitive soul, were hushed to rest. My soul was in such intimate communion with its Maker that it only longed to go home.'" And so it is with those whose lives are linked in glorious spiritual oneness with Christ; to them the great longing is to meet Him face to face, that the union may find its full consummation and fruition.

I am the Lord's! Yes; body, soul and spirit,
O seal them irrevocably Thine;
As Thou, Beloved, in Thy grace and fulness
For ever and for evermore art mine.

"My Beloved is mine, and I am His." This is the language of possession, of proprietorship. It spells death to the life of self-guidance, self-gratification, self-glorying, and self-government. It is the mark of ownership, the seal of relationship that stamps me for ever as *His own*. This means that my thoughts are *His*; my affections are *His*; my talents are *His*; my time is *His*; my money is *His*; I have surrendered every right over my life; I have willed myself away to another; "I am not my own." The very love-gifts that grace my life proclaim me *His*. Those holy spiritual adornments that cover the shame of my nakedness are the earnest of the glory which awaits those who are *His*.

Everyone has some one or some thing to which heart and mind are given – their *master passion*. With Sir Isaac Newton it was science. His days and nights were given to his diagrams, his mathematical table, and his telescopes. With Lloyd Garrison the master passion was the freedom of the slave. With John B. Gough the rescue of his fellow-men from strong drink. But Zinzendorf said, "I have but one passion – it is He." And with St. Paul – "To me to live is Christ." Oh the rapture of being thus wholly absorbed in Him! Of being so completely *His!*

His the life that triumphs over death, which I take for my body "moment by moment." *His* the wonderful "newness of energy" which is always sufficient. When perhaps distraught by a thousand vexing and perplexing cares; when the nerves are all at such a painful tension, and one is threatened by physical collapse, then *His* are the arms upon which I lean my weakness. *His* the Spirit that I take for my power day after day. *His* the joy that continually adorns and equips the otherwise barren ministry, making it fruitful, fragrant, and fresh. *His* the touch that steadies the soul when it might become unduly biased or unbalanced, giving to it a beautiful and becoming evenness. *His* the love that flows in an unceasing stream through the yielded channel, enabling it to "count the cross a prize." *His* the hand that wipes away the burning tears, and calms the fevered brow. *His* the fire that burns its way through my life, making it luminous and lustrous for Him. *His* the abundant and abiding provision that always adequately meets my need. *His* the deep, sweet peace that fills my soul and garrisons my mind against every sinister suggestion from the foe.

155

Love's Miracles

And so it is all *His*! *His* the battle; *His* the song; *His* the victory; *His* the healing; *His* the glory. Who can tell the unfathomable blessedness of daily realising that we are *His*? *His* inheritance! It is just the surest and safest way of living a life that is free from worldliness. This glad consciousness will prevent heart-wandering, and keep us simply "glued" to Him. Oh, the honour, the dignity of really being *His*! The wondrous privilege of access to *His* presence – of listening to *His* voice. I belong to the King, therefore I must be kingly in my conduct. I am part of the bride-elect of the Lamb, consequently I must deport myself as becometh such a high and holy calling. My body is the shrine in which *His* life is resident, and through which it may become manifest, the "earthen vessel" through which He delights to pour Himself upon the thirsty world.

"St. Francis of Assisi, the Methodist of the thirteenth century, was once watched by one who loved him well, that he might learn from his master how to pray, as his master had learnt from Him who taught His disciples in the days of old; and when he watched with indelicate intrusion, but with a holy intent, this was all he discovered: over and over again the saint was saying, with bowed head and clasped hands, the name of Jesus." Oh the everlasting wonder of that name! Oh the inexpressible beauty that holds me prisoner – that captures the homage of my heart – that lays me prostrate upon the altar of dedication – that constrains me to sing –

His for ever, only His;
Who the Lord and me shall part?
Ah, with what a rest of bliss,
Christ can fill the loving heart.